The Essential Wood-Fired Pizza Cookbook

THE ESSENTIAL
WOOD-FIRED
PIZZA
COOKBOOK

Recipes and Techniques
from My Wood-Fired Oven

ANTHONY TASSINELLO

Photography by Kelly Ishikawa
Styling by Rod Hipskind

ROCKRIDGE
PRESS

For general information on our other products and services or to obtain technical support, please contact our Customer Care Department within the United States at (866) 744-2665, or outside the United States at (510) 253-0500.

Rockridge Press publishes its books in a variety of electronic and print formats. Some content that appears in print may not be available in electronic books, and vice versa.

TRADEMARKS: Rockridge Press and the Rockridge Press logo are trademarks or registered trademarks of Callisto Media Inc. and/or its affiliates, in the United States and other countries, and may not be used without written permission. All other trademarks are the property of their respective owners. Rockridge Press is not associated with any product or vendor mentioned in this book.

Photography © 2016 by Kelly Ishikawa
Styling by Rod Hipskind
Illustrations by Tom Bingham

ISBN: Print 978-1-62315-724-1
eBook 978-1-62315-725-8

For Mom and Dad,
Frances and Bruno,
you are the fire
in my life

CONTENTS

INTRODUCTION

VOLUMES HAVE BEEN WRITTEN about the pleasures of the table and the meaning of cuisine in our lives. If we pause and consider food as a medium, it has for centuries defined our celebrations and lamentations, but the days between the festivals and holidays also carry weight. These small moments, too, can have deep meaning and bring us sustenance.

The rise of the kitchen as a hub for family activity has not gone unnoticed by modern social scientists. As smart home technology has blossomed, the kitchen has been elevated as well. Rain-filled, rusty grills are giving way to showpieces for culinary adventure. Consequently, we begin to see former luxury items, such as outdoor kitchens and wood-burning pizza ovens, included in many new construction projects and remodels.

For the established homeowner with culinary ambition, the addition of a wood-fired pizza oven can unlock an atlas of edible adventures. To put it simply, people are revisiting the joys of gathering friends and family to reconnect, meaningfully, over a delicious home-cooked meal. What was once looked upon as a burden—shopping, cooking, and serving—has more recently become a gift of gratitude. The idea of creating edible memories is leaving an indelible mark on our collective consciousness and our palates alike.

Over the past decade, a wave of enthusiasm about ingredients and their pedigree has seen "family meal night" expand exponentially. A new breed of do-it-yourself, home-based, artisanal foodies has drawn the awareness of what we eat and how we eat it out of restaurant kitchens and placed it squarely in the capable hands of 21st-century home cooks. It's no surprise, then, that high-tech cooking gadgets now dominate the retail landscape; novice chefs are encouraged to create signature dishes using odd techniques that achieve scientific results.

Have we lost our way? This story of cooking comes not only from the nourishment we gain, but also from the pleasure derived from the sights, sounds, and smells of those pedigreed ingredients being transformed. Gone are the heady aromas: hijacked, vacuum-packed, and plunged underwater. Certainly, there will always be room for experimentation and culinary invention, but leave that to the chefs in lab coats. This is an exploration of a more primitive method of cooking.

Fear not—we won't entirely abandon the modern ethos of food preparation. Instead, we will explore an area of our gastronomic past that is experiencing a bit of a renaissance. The bonus is that this way of cooking does not inhibit our culinary senses, but emboldens them. Let me (re)introduce you to a celebration of fiery wood-oven cookery.

If I had to choose one method of cooking, nothing seems to quite capture my attention more than live fire. Maybe it's a primal instinct, innate and hardwired in all of us, that dates to when our ancestors first "tamed" the flame. Fire is wildly alluring, with its dancing, unpredictable patterns, smells and crackles, sparks and smoke, glowing coal beds and radiant heat. Honestly, it's slightly intimidating, too. Tending a fire can take focus, but when done with confidence and poise, it's a not-so-gentle reminder of humanity's greatest triumph over nature.

Beginning with the basics, we'll explore the different types of ovens, fire-building practices, and suggestions for how to alter your oven performance, as well as a variety of cooking techniques. We'll look at the when and the where of preparing recipes based on your choice of fire styles. We will also explore an array of cookware, fuel types, and necessary equipment to help streamline your cooking experience for delicious success.

More than 85 recipes will tempt you to explore the full range of capabilities that your wood-burning pizza oven can handle. In-depth reviews of ingredients are coupled with tips on how to make a perfect pizza for anything from a casual midweek supper to a full-blown wood oven celebration.

From the classically simple, perfect Margherita pizza and everybody's favorite pepperoni pie, we will gradually progress to more exciting and challenging recipes that showcase different uses for your oven. Included are recipes for every night of the week, as well as special occasions. Together we will transform and elevate humble ingredients in all manner of savory dishes, from appetizers and entrées to sides, and even a few sweet offerings. You will also find additional tips and insights that will have you turning again and again to your hearth. Let's get started!

PART ONE

A WOOD-FIRED OVEN ROMANCE

1 FIRE UP THE OVEN

IF YOU HAVE MADE the exciting decision to embark on the culinary journey that is wood-fired oven cookery, congratulations! You are in for an enlightening and delicious experience, a bit of hard work, and, ultimately, an increased acumen when working with live fire. If you are considering adding a wood-burning oven to your property, I hope the knowledge contained in this book will convince you to go ahead and do it.

For the current oven owner, I've got good news and better news. The good news is there are no shortcuts when learning the nuances of your particular oven. This is a craft that you will grow into, one with no particular timetable. Why is this good news? Because you can expect fine results, and an abundance of entertainment, even during your earliest attempts at cooking with fire. And the better news is that whether you choose to fire your oven several times a year or several times a month, you will constantly be building on the knowledge you gained from the previous session.

A TIME-TESTED TRADITION

Perhaps the reason we refer to the Old World as "old" has to do with the cooking methods that have filtered through to modern times. We can only speculate, of course, but imagine the first few savory morsels that were exposed to live fire and how our ancestors came to prefer them. Maybe it was accidental—an overlooked scrap of meat dropped near the hearth and seared on a hot rock. From that moment on, our path was altered. Nothing is older than cooking with fire, and using ovens to prolong the energy in our fuel was a logical progression on the learning curve. The less time spent gathering firewood and burning through precious calories, the greater your chances of surviving another day.

Pottery shards discovered in southeast China dating back nearly 20,000 years contain remnants of soot, presumably from cooking fires. Farming and agriculture took root several millennia later, implying that these were people on the move, carrying their cooking vessels as they followed food sources.

As civilization progressed and cultures evolved, it became evident that oven cookery was cross-cultural. Examples exist of ancient Egyptians using clay pots, a possible predecessor to the Indian tandoor oven. Simple by nature, a fire is built in the base of an open-topped vessel and the interior walls are used as the cooking medium, capturing heat while smoke escapes. This kind of oven was effective and easy to construct, but rather inefficient in how much heat it retained.

The Roman Empire took oven technology several steps further. In fact, most commercially available wood-fired ovens on the market today operate using some or all of the techniques used by those ancient Roman bakers. They use three main scientific principles of cooking with fire: refractory heat from the oven floor, radiant heat from the fire source, and convection heat created by the curve of the interior dome.

TYPES OF WOOD-FIRED OVENS

A dazzling array of ovens exists, constructed from a host of natural and manmade materials or a hybrid of both. I've seen ovens that ingeniously repurpose urban waste (car tires, old washing machines, even dryer lint) and integrate those materials in very resourceful ways. If budget is an issue, these are ways to trim the fat on your oven construction project.

We'll take a look at some of the more popular types of wood-fired ovens on the market and highlight their strengths and weaknesses. Some ancient oven designs still have 21st-century applications, like the durable cob oven. If you prefer a more finished, stand-alone structure, maybe a kit or a brick oven is the ultimate option. In the end, though, it's about deciding what is best for you and your budget, and how the project fits your construction footprint and the workload you are willing to shoulder. Whichever you choose, this book will help you cook delicious meals for the life of your new oven.

Clay/Cob Ovens

A brilliant example of an ancient building design that still has modern applications is the cob oven. The term "cob" has English origins and refers to a sustainable building material that is an amalgam of clay, sand, water, and a fibrous tensile material, usually straw. Cob, also known as adobe, has been in continuous use for centuries as a structural building material, and in fact has changed very little, other than in its aesthetics and preservation techniques.

Some of the qualities of cob as a construction material are its fire resistance, malleability, and long-term stability. Organic by nature, it readily holds heat, can be fabricated by hand, and is economical to produce.

Cob or earth ovens are also known as Roman-style ovens. They consist of a single domed chamber with an opening in front and a direct heat source (in this case, fire) within. A chimney may or may not be part of this type of oven. Cob ovens rely on the method of cooking that is generally described throughout this book: proximity to an intense heat source and reliance on convection, reflection, and refraction to get the job done.

Personally, I prefer this oven-building technique, and many do-it-yourselfers agree with me. While it lacks the professional finished look of some of the pricier imported kit ovens, it nearly matches them in the cooking department. Plus, it is a project that can be done manually—and that has intrinsic value to me, especially in an increasingly prepackaged society.

Brick Ovens

Growing up in New Jersey as I did, we would often go out for pizza rather than have it delivered. Locally, it seemed that every tavern or Italian restaurant advertised authentic brick-oven baked pies. At the time, I assumed that was how all pizza was made: well done, long-cooked, crisp and doughy all at once. It would come to the table presliced in massive wedges, the whole round measuring almost two feet across. You chose a piece, slid it off the pan, and a web of mozzarella stretching all the way to your plate followed; a folded, heavy slice, pooled with oily, cheesy goodness in one hand, and a fistful of napkins in the other.

Brick ovens are an ideal way to cook pizza, and not just the classic Neapolitan style. A deep cooking chamber lined with masonry brick and heated either indirectly (a firebox) or directly (gas or electricity) acts like the dome structure of a classic cob oven. The masonry can be a variety of materials, including firebrick, concrete, or stone.

Traditional coal-fired ovens fall into the brick oven or masonry category as well, and were also lauded as an ideal way to cook pizzas in the Northeast and, later, nationwide. Popular from the 19th century on, a two-chamber system was used. The first, the firebox, was filled with burning coal and generated heat that flowed through a flue and filled a secondary baking chamber. Anthracite coal was plentiful and cheap, and still is. It also burns very hot, making it a top choice for fueling pizza and bread ovens.

In cooking terms, "convection" means the transfer of thermal heat away from the combustion source, either through gravity or, in this case, air currents caused by the oven's draft. "Reflection" means the heat produced by the combustion of fire that is reflected off the inner surfaces of the oven, then reflected onto the food cooking in the oven. "Refraction" means the energy that is produced by the combustion of the fire that is transferred to the insulative layers of the oven. The stored energy is ultimately diffused, but during the process is refracted onto the contents of the oven.

BUILDING A WOOD-FIRED OVEN

Considering building a wood-fired oven? Here are several criteria to consider. First, think about safety. Then the location (indoor or outdoor), followed by price point, and construction methods. The type of oven you choose will dictate further considerations such as material type, style, and size. Perhaps the biggest decision is whether to do it all yourself or buy a kit. Both options offer challenges as well as rewards throughout the planning and completion process.

Fortunately, there is opportunity for a hands-on experience at most every price point. On the high end, there are reputable manufacturers that will guide you through every step of the process. They typically offer a range of design options, accessories, assembly services, and even cooking classes. Pricier options may include factory assembly of an imported oven, delivery, and complete installation, right down to finished masonry. On the lower end of the price spectrum, there are simple ovens that can be made by hand in several days (aided by an eager group of friends) using very low-cost materials.

Ultimately, building your own oven is a labor of love; you'll exercise full control over the design and construction. Personally, I prefer this. But beware: There is no oven hotline to call if you encounter problems—and you surely will. Trial and error is part of the process.

My friends wouldn't exactly call me handy. However, I managed to construct an attractive, functional oven at home that churns out delicious food night after night. I'm quite proud of that, and you can share in the gratification, too. Often the first question I get from guests is, "Did you make that?" With pride I answer, "With a few friends, yes."

Other Types of Ovens

There is a range of alternative oven styles, including gas- and electric-powered floor ovens and even ovens that use the structural aspects of Roman-style ovens but are fueled by natural gas. The coal-oven model, whereby two chambers are used and the heat is indirect, seems too commercial and bulky for the home, although these ovens are effective.

GET TO KNOW YOUR OVEN

If you chose to build your own wood-burning pizza oven, great. In the process of putting it together, you probably got to know all its parts and functions. If you purchased a pre-fab kit or had it built for you, it's wise to take some time to become familiar with the oven's functionality. There are three basic components to your oven: foundation, floor, and dome. Understanding the role of each will help you maintain the overall performance of your oven.

How It Works

So what exactly is going on in there that makes delicious pizza in less than five minutes? Let's get a little technical for a moment, and then we'll get back to eating and drinking.

Your oven is a marvelous creation that harnesses some inherent scientific properties of airflow, refraction, reflection, and heat. We'll call that the environment—and I'll get back to it in a moment.

The three components of the wood-fired oven all play a cooperative role in its function. Beginning at the bottom, the foundation provides height for an easy work experience and structural support for the floor and dome. Often it doubles as a conveniently located shelter to keep your wood handy and dry, an arm's length away. Additionally, for some types of ovens, such as cob, it is essential that ground moisture doesn't creep up into the oven floor. Elevating the structure prevents that.

The floor is the heating element of the oven. It's usually made of fire-brick or a poured slab of some sort that holds the intense heat fed into it from the fire. A well-insulated floor can stay hot long enough to cook dozens of pizzas before the fire should be raked back over and the oven is reheated.

Finally, there's the dome structure. Depending on the design of your oven, the dome may not be visible from the exterior. Notice the interior shape, the curvature. The height of the dome is in direct proportion to the size of the oven's opening and creates a "draw," or positive airflow, that in turn circulates heat and carries smoke up and out via the chimney or mouth.

The Environment

Despite the fact that there is only a single cooking chamber in your oven, you can create several different cooking environments. Varying the intensity of the fire is a quick and easy way to control how fast food will cook. Abundant flames give off abundant heat; spreading the fire out will limit the concentration and produce less heat.

Your oven uses a few simple techniques to maintain cooking temperature. The main one is refraction, where the energy produced by burning wood is captured in the floor, walls, and surrounding insulative layers of the oven. One way to measure the refractive capability of your oven is to check it the morning after you use it. Feel the warmth?

Reflection is the heat being generated by the fire bouncing off the curvature of the inner dome and down onto the food you're cooking. The oven is a super-heated, extremely dry, harsh environment, filled with heat energy. It's the draw—or the draft, if you prefer—that creates airflow and merges with that energy to yield convection, which is the transfer of heat via the motion of air. This draw is created by the heat that comes from the fire, since, as we know, heat rises.

Try this experiment the next time you have a pizza that you would like to be just a bit more well done. Scoop the pie up with your metal peel, then carefully lift it toward the inner top of the dome. Hold it in place for a few moments. That brief lift takes the pizza out of the cooler

Location, location, location. Choosing the right spot for your pizza oven is not so easy. If it's outdoors, consider a number of factors: proximity to your main kitchen, aesthetics within your landscape design, and, above all, safety.

layers of air below and places it in a highly convected super-hot zone. Check out those blistering, bubbling toppings!

Some of the recipes in this book require slower cooking methods. One simple way of achieving that is minimizing the size of the fire, but you can also move items closer to or farther away from the heat source to control the temperature. Imagine a series of rings around the fire, with the inner ring being the hottest, the outer the coolest. It is astonishing how much temperature variation there is in that chamber. Don't discount the value of using the doorway as a cooler cooking alternative, either. Half- and quarter-sheet pans are invaluable for this type of cookery; just be sure to rotate them often for even doneness.

Oven Cleaning and Maintenance

Many of the ovens available to consumers today have easy-care guidelines and relatively low maintenance. Masonry and adobe don't need a great deal of upkeep. What you'll mostly be dealing with is the best way to keep the work surfaces clean and, in some cases, to protect the structure from the elements. I use several readily available non-toxic all-purpose cleaners for the exterior mantle in between uses.

There are, however, a few things you can expect to see as your oven becomes well worn. Discoloration from wood smoke is common around the mouth of the oven and can be wiped away with a damp cloth from time to time, but will always persist. Hairline fissures and subtle cracking are a natural occurrence from heating and cooling. Generally, they don't detract from the overall appearance, but a fresh coat of stucco every few years can clean up any blemishes. Large cracks are a problem and may represent a greater structural problem; it's best to contact the builder or manufacturer for how to proceed.

Fire is a great sterilizer and most often burns away any food spills. Occasionally, clean the floor of the oven with a stiff wire brush (when the oven is appropriately cool), and remove all spent ashes and unburned wood before starting a new fire.

THE FUEL

We know that fire requires oxygen plus a fuel source to burn, so airflow and good wood are crucial to a successful fire. The fuel you choose for your oven falls into two categories: what you use to fire up the oven and the fuel you cook with. Depending on the size and type of wood-fired oven you have, the time it takes to get to cooking temperature will vary. I prefer to use lesser cuts of wood (such as pine or kindling or any wood that doesn't have chemicals in it) to bring up the temperature, and reserve the hardwoods, fruitwoods, and vine cuttings for cooking.

Sourcing Wood

Finding a reputable source for the fuel for your wood-fired oven can be difficult and expensive. Beware of classified and online ads offering cheap firewood. Anyone with a chainsaw and a pickup truck can call themselves a firewood dealer. You're likely to get unseasoned, mixed woods, cut to varying lengths or rounds, and quite possibly all of the above. Firewood has to season for a period of time to allow most of the moisture to escape and dry. Unseasoned "green" wood will hardly burn at all—if you can even manage to light it. Green wood is inefficient; it won't produce much heat, and often doesn't burn all the way through.

Remember this rule: Not all wood is firewood. In general, I prefer three types of wood to burn for cooking: hardwood, fruitwood, and vine cuttings. Northern California, where I live, offers an abundance of oak, over a dozen species of which are ideal for cooking. When properly seasoned and split to manageable lengths, oak provides ease of oven operation, long burn time, and little smoke. If you don't have an oak source near you, ask around town and at the farmers' market, or seek out a reputable firewood dealer that you can visit. They'll fill you in on what makes the finest cooking wood in your area.

A great alternative to hardwood is fruitwood. I'm speaking of woods such as almond, walnut, cherry, or even plum. If there are fruit orchards or farms in your area, ask about sourcing firewood directly. I like using fruitwood because it is sustainable; normally, at the end of a tree's life, it no longer bears fruit and needs to be replaced. Using this

Take the time to experiment with different fire intensities, and test all the corners of your oven. Each is unique and contains relative hot spots. I use a thick slice of bread to gauge all the different zones: Where does it burn? Where is it gently toasting?

type of wood completes the life cycle of the tree, in my opinion. Seasoned fruitwood, like hardwood, doesn't contain a lot of oil, making it ideal for cooking.

Be sure to avoid softwoods such as most pine species, and especially eucalyptus. They burn too rapidly and are filled with sap. Oily or sappy wood produces an abundance of creosote and will gum up your chimney. Additionally, it releases black particulate-filled smoke into the air. Constantly feeding the fire, coupled with minimal coal bed production, leads to a waste of money and resources. All are reasons to avoid cooking with softwoods.

Finally, if you can find vine cuttings, specifically grape vines, these are ideal for grilling or using in the wood oven. Dried vine cuttings are generally available after the grape harvests begin at the end of the summer and end in the fall; visit a few local vineyards and inquire at the tasting room. Common wine varietals that we all know, such as chardonnay and cabernet sauvignon, produce finger-thick vines that, when dried and burned, produce a fragrant floral note. Vine cuttings burn bright but brief, so I never burn them by themselves. Rather, I add them to an established fire for a kick of heat and a note of smoke in the final moments of cooking. Soaking them briefly in water will prolong their burn time, but not by much.

Firing Your Oven

The engine room of your wood oven experience is, of course, fire, so understanding how to create it safely and monitor its progress will only help reward you with delicious food. Building a fire has risen to an art form in recent times. Perhaps it's a testament to our cultural advancement that something that was so essential to our early survival has lately been filtered through the lens of lifestyle magazines. However you choose to view it, a well-made fire is a delight to behold and takes practice to execute. That being said, you can experience all the simple joys of your oven with an uncomplicated fire-building technique.

Choose hardwoods, such as oak, hickory, maple, and birch, for cooking, and avoid resinous or soft woods. Trees such as pine and eucalyptus, while plentiful, contain far too much sap and oils. Burning these resins creates an acrid smoke, leading to an unpleasant flavor in your cooked food.

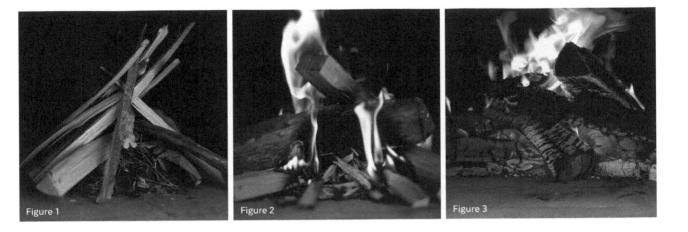

Figure 1 Figure 2 Figure 3

This section assumes your oven has been sufficiently cured and is ready for a full fire, followed by a prolonged cooking session. Follow the manufacturer's instructions on how to properly cure your oven before using it for the first time. Improper curing can lead to cracking, warping, and a possible collapse of the structure, so be sure to follow those initial steps—do so and your oven will last for years.

It is best to light the fire right on the spot you'll eventually be cooking on, and then shift it to one side after it is well established. Begin by lighting a small fire consisting of kindling and a bit of newspaper, sawdust, dry pinecones, or something similar, about 6 to 8 inches inside the mouth of the oven. Fire needs oxygen to burn, and one reason for your oven's shape is to provide an ample flow of oxygen. The general idea is to stack the kindling in a crosshatch or pyramid pattern to provide space for oxygen to flow through (see Figure 1). The fire will most likely start out smoky and then, as the draft takes over, it will become more efficient and stop smoking. Gradually feed the starter fire by adding larger and larger pieces of kindling (see Figure 2).

As the fire burns, monitor it from time to time and add a log here or there, stacking appropriately. The goal is to create space through stacking that allows air to flow around the log you are adding, so stacking perpendicular is better than parallel, or you can offset logs to create air pockets. You want to create a well-burning, hot fire about 18 inches wide and 18 inches deep. This should take about 45 minutes to an

SAFETY TIPS

Safety guidelines appear many times throughout this book. Keeping everyone safe, including yourself, while enjoying your wood-fired oven is the foundation for years of pleasure your oven will provide. Beginning with construction safety and continuing through to fire building and finally cooking, observe these cautions:

- **Cooking with live fire is intended for adults.** However, take the opportunity to teach young children how to properly respect fire and you'll have taught them an important life lesson.

- **Handle with care.** Cooking vessels such as cast iron skillets and clay pots retain heat (a desirable effect), but may look deceptively cool to the touch.

- **Obey local laws regarding burning wood fires.** Here in California we have many days throughout the year when weather patterns create unsafe air quality. Adding smoke particulates to the air only compounds the problem for people with respiratory problems such as asthma. Reschedule your pizza party until weather permits and help create a safer environment.

- **Source your wood from a reputable supplier.** Make sure it hasn't been treated with harmful chemicals and doesn't contain nails. You're cooking with it, after all; it should have the same pedigree as your ingredients.

- **Never use an accelerant to start a fire in your wood oven.** Lighter fluid has no place in this style of cooking, and produces odd chemical flavors in the food. Instead, use twigs or dry kindling, sawdust, dry pinecones, and/or minimal amounts of crumpled newspaper to ignite the fire. Later, for cooking, choose dry, seasoned split wood for your fire. This minimizes smoke, as wet wood only smolders.

hour. If a log rolls out of place or seems to be burning inefficiently, use a poker to lift, adjust, or stoke the blaze.

About an hour or so into the burning process, you can start to build the coal bed (see Figure 3). Carefully add one large split log at this point and let the fire intensify. Not only is the fire creating floor heat, it is simultaneously heating the dome. Continue tending the fire for two to three hours, depending on the size and type of your oven, or until you get an internal temperature of around 800° to 1,000°F.

When the oven is sufficiently heated, use a fire rake to move the burning mass carefully to one side of the oven. You'll need open space on the floor to cook your pizza. Left side or right side is up to you, but you are trying to maximize space while creating plenty of air and heat flow. Confine the fire as you brush away all the embers and clear the floor of dust. Be quick and deliberate when brushing—extended time in a hot oven shortens the lifespan of your equipment. The oven is now ready for cooking.

TOOLS OF THE TRADE

To operate your oven safely and successfully, you will need to acquaint yourself with an array of tools. As with most hobbies, you can geek out on every new trinket that hits the market—and spend a fortune doing so. But before you do that, let's visit a few "must haves."

My goal is to streamline the cooking process and ensure great results while minimizing cleanup. A good *pizzaiolo* (pizza chef) can create legendary pies with just a few simple utensils, and you will, too. I imagine that over time you will develop your own ideas about what is considered indispensible and what is superfluous. In the meantime, I'll offer some advice from a chef's perspective.

Knife skills are important when it comes to prepping ingredients, but not imperative. I'm going to assume that if you are interested in cooking, you can handle the basics: A chef's knife and a paring knife will take you far.

Most ovens on the market today are relatively efficient, achieving and maintaining a consistent temperature within two to three hours of firing. If you are going to the effort of lighting a fire and making a batch of dough for your own dinner, why not invite a group of friends or even a few neighbors to dinner?

What You Need

CAST IRON COOKWARE. Nothing holds the heat quite like a great piece of American-made cast iron cookware. When properly seasoned, it can handle anything you can cook up in the wood oven. It is durable, convenient to use, and stylish in its simplicity. Caution: Collecting cast iron is a slippery slope. I find myself stopping at garage sales and antique shops whenever possible with the hopes of finding a piece I don't have (and didn't know I needed). My two favorite brands are Wagner and Griswold; you may have to pay a premium, but they will still be cooking long after you and I are gone.

CAZUELA POTTERY. This glazed or enameled pottery, typically from South America (*cazuela* is Spanish for "cooking pot"), is stunningly beautiful and particularly useful. I look for functionality in cookware, and the range of sizes of these vessels is limitless. The ability to go from oven to table minimizes cleanup and makes easy work of serving large groups. Find them in South American markets or online. Follow the curing instructions before their initial use and they'll last a long time.

DOUGH STORAGE CONTAINERS. Any large, clear plastic container with a tight-fitting lid will do. Cambro is a brand I prefer because it is restaurant grade, durable, and marked with measurements on the side. The 8-quart and 12-quart sizes should serve your needs for refrigerating finished yet unrisen doughs overnight.

PIZZA CUTTER. A simple wheeled pizza cutter is essential. Make quick work of portioning your pies and save your kitchen knives for chopping and slicing.

BENCH SCRAPER. This stainless steel tool is indispensible for gathering and portioning dough from your work surface. It's also helpful for removing dried or sticky bits from counters, making cleanup go faster.

METAL PEEL. This is one tool you'll hardly put down. Become familiar with just how many tasks you can complete inside the oven with this long-handled, spatula-like instrument. Turning pizzas for even cooking is its general function, but you can also use your peel to arrange cazuelas front to back, lift a rogue log that has tumbled off the fire, and a lot more.

WOODEN PEEL. A thin, long-handled peel is used solely for transferring your uncooked pizzas and calzones from your prep area to the oven. Invest in two or three to get started, so you can build multiple pies at the same time.

STRAW BROOM. I recommend a cheap, long-handled straw broom for quickly—and I mean *quickly*—brushing the oven floor clean of ashes before firing your first pizza of the day (after you've got your oven going). Smoky, charred pizza is delicious; baking soot into your pie is not.

FIRE EXTINGUISHER. It is a good idea to have a small fire extinguisher on hand just in case of an emergency. Remember, you are dealing with live fire. Better to have it and not need it than need it and not have it.

POKER. You will need to poke and prod the fire to maintain airflow. A long-handled metal fireplace poker will help you stoke the fire properly and move logs with ease.

WIRE BRUSH. A long-handled wire brush is useful for brushing away any ingredients from the cook surface that may have bubbled over or toppled off your pizzas. Occasionally, a pie will spring a leak. A few strokes of the wire brush and you are right back at it.

SHEET PANS. These are an absolute must for pizza oven prep and cooking. Invest in heavy-duty rimmed trays known as half sheets and quarter sheets. (A full sheet most likely won't fit in your oven.) You will use them endlessly for things like proofing (the fermentation process the dough goes through as it rests), roasting ingredients for toppings, and baking focaccia.

PIZZA PANS. Round aluminum pizza pans make great landing pads for finished, piping-hot pizzas. A few passes of the pizza cutter and you have an instant serving platter, or a way to transfer the pie to a more formal serving plate quickly and easily.

For the Master

FOUR-QUART STAND MIXER. In my opinion, one of the most essential tools for any well-outfitted kitchen is a heavy-duty 4-quart electric stand mixer. I like the KitchenAid brand for its ease of use and added attachments such as the pasta sheeter and the meat grinder. I have included it here because while you can make any of the dough recipes in this book by hand, it is far easier to use a stand mixer. Go ahead and buy an extra work bowl and all the attachments while you are at it; you will use them.

MANDOLINE. A great addition to your cooking arsenal is a razor-sharp French slicing tool known as a mandoline. It is essentially a very thin, stationary blade held in place in an adjustable plastic shelf. The mandoline enables you to quickly and evenly slice vegetables with precision.

MORTAR AND PESTLE. A mortar and pestle is a rudimentary kitchen tool used for pounding ingredients into pastes and powders. It consists of two pieces: a footed, heavy stone bowl, usually with a rough interior to help grind ingredients, and a rounded weighty baton used for mashing. Part apothecary, part Neanderthal in its simplicity, it allows you to achieve quick results that are unrivaled compared with other kitchen gadgets.

DIGITAL KITCHEN SCALE. A small battery-powered digital scale is an indispensable tool in my kitchen. I prefer to weigh my dough ingredients rather than use a dry cup measure, because flour weights can fluctuate a great deal depending on the milling process. That's why in this book, you'll find weights as well as standard cup measurements for flour in all the dough recipes.

LASER THERMOMETER. One of the great new inventions to hit the market is the laser thermometer. It's a small battery-powered gun that fires an infrared laser and gives you an instant LED temperature reading. It's addictive and fun to scan the walls, floor, and ceiling of your fiery oven and marvel at the extreme heat. Is it necessary? No. But it is helpful to know floor temperatures when you are making a recipe that requires the baking to be a bit more moderate.

CAST IRON GRILL GRATE. If producing crispy wood-fired pizzas is not enough for you, buy a narrow-footed cast iron grill for grilling foods in the mouth of your pizza oven. Rake a bed of hot coals beneath the grate and cook anything you like without ever firing up the Weber.

2 PIZZA NIGHT

IF YOU ARE ABOUT TO EMBARK on the maiden voyage of your wood-fired oven, it is a momentous occasion—the nexus of hard work, thoughtful planning, and detailed food preparation. Even if you are a seasoned veteran of cooking with fire, you still need to consider all the details for making pizza night a tasty success. Get ready for an interactive, free-flowing food celebration with fire as the guest star.

HOW TO BUILD THE PERFECT PIZZA

The pride and excitement of harnessing this source of heat and live energy as it transforms humble ingredients into delectable bites within minutes hasn't been lost on me, even after firing hundreds, if not thousands, of pizzas. You'll notice the same thrill on your guests' faces. As you go about the steps of shaping the dough and building the pie, enthusiasm builds. Then come those first few dramatic moments when the dough springs to life against the blistering oven floor. It sets and bubbles against the intense heat, then is quickly rescued before the extreme fire over-bakes the pie. Everyone watches as it is sliced and garnished, then proudly presented. Friends vie for a slice, and politeness takes a backseat as guests eye their favorite piece and dig in. Those first few steamy, crispy, smoky bites of a perfect pizza cooked before their eyes have them ready for the next pie, and the next, all coming from your wood-fired oven. You should probably open some more wine—the party is just getting on track.

The Ingredients

Everyone knows the old saying, "You are what you eat," but it has also been said, "You are what you eat, eats." And so it goes that we need to strive for better ingredients and sustainability surrounding the dinner table. Consumer sentiment, not supply and demand, drives the choices we have at the grocery store.

Take a moment to think of the food trends we're currently experiencing in the early 21st century. Kale is in everything, coconut water is about to supplant actual water, and chia seeds have leaped out of the flowerpot and into our snacks. These changes are partially due to marketing, but mainly due to eaters embracing fresh produce and healthy snacks. By making informed choices about what we buy, we can change what is readily available to us.

When you're making a list of ingredients to build the perfect pizza, start from the ground up—the essential building blocks of what makes a memorable pie. We've already discussed the proper wood for the fire;

now let's talk about stocking the larder. Your guests might not see what goes on behind the scenes of your pizza extravaganza, but I assure you they will be the benefactors of your informed shopping. Here are a few staples to get you up and running.

EXTRA-VIRGIN OLIVE OIL. This goes in everything from the doughs to the sauces to the toppings. Don't break the bank, but do avoid the discount warehouse brands. California is producing affordable, quality olive oil these days for a lower price point.

FLOUR. Choose organic when possible. A good all-purpose white will serve most needs. Then, find a source for the more boutique grains like rye, 100 percent whole-wheat, semolina, and other flours that are used in the recipes in this book. In my opinion, imported 00 flour is essential for making the majority of doughs in this book. Known simply as "double zero," this flour is a revelation to the home pizza maker. The "00" refers to the texture of the flour. Italian flours are classified by numbers according to how finely they are ground—the roughest is 1, and the finest is 00. A finer grind and lower gluten content make this an absolute favorite of mine for both pizzas and calzones, and when combined with other flours, it provides a great balance to your dough. Until recently, 00 was not readily available in the United States, but it can now be found in specialty stores and online. One popular brand is Caputo, which comes in small red bags. Look for the "00" on the bag and you'll be fine, regardless of the producer.

TOMATO SAUCE. Please don't buy sauce in a jar! It takes just minutes to create a simple, fresh tomato sauce worthy of your pizza party. If you've invested two days making dough from scratch, don't cut corners on the sauce.

SEASONAL INGREDIENTS. This is more of an overarching philosophy than a single suggestion. Without getting into specifics, let the seasons dictate your menus for you. Unless you live in Chile, don't reach for asparagus in January. Instead, buy what your local farmers are bringing to market. One way to get the best of the seasons is to seek out and join a CSA, or community-supported agriculture program. You'll pay a flat fee and receive a variety of produce weekly or monthly, so you will quickly learn what thrives in your area and when.

Need-to-Know Tips

These tips will help you craft the perfect pizza. They will keep your cooking running smoothly and allow you to focus on your guests.

Let the flour fly! You don't have to toss a pie dough in the air to achieve the ideal shape, but it sure helps. Centrifugal force pulls the dough outward into a disk, so your hands don't have to. How cool will you look when your perfectly stretched dough takes flight, twirls, and then lands back in your hands? Answer: Bravissimo!

- Perfect pizza comes from hand shaping. Avoid relying on a rolling pin to create a thin crust. To get a feel for properly proofed dough, stretch it by hand.

- If the dough seems unwilling to maintain its shape on your peel and is noticeably contracting, wait about five minutes for the gluten to relax and then gently stretch it a bit more. I'm generally not too concerned with shape; round or oval tastes the same but thickness counts. Thin to win is my mantra.

- Less is more when it comes to saucing and topping pizzas. Weighty, wet ingredients cause the dough to steam rather than spring to life. A limp, undercooked pie just will not do.

- Finish like a pro. Keep a small ramekin of chopped garlic covered in olive oil on your prep station. Finish the cooked pizza by brushing the crust with a thin coat of garlic oil for added flavor and a glossy crust.

- The best pizzas are made in a hot, bright oven, meaning a fully engaged fire with flames that roll over the dome and a fully heated floor. Add a slender split log directly to the fire if there is no active flame, and let it ignite before baking a pie.

- After 10 to 15 pizzas, most ovens will experience a drop in floor temperature. Reheat the floor by raking the embers back over the cooking surface and allow it to stand for 10 minutes. Push the fire aside, add a thin log to the embers, and allow it to ignite; then resweep the floor and resume turning out crispy pies.

- Some ingredients need to be cooked before topping a raw pizza; they won't properly finish in the short amount of time the dough spends in the oven. Precook thinly sliced vegetables such as potatoes and eggplant. Other ingredients, such as greens and mushrooms, can contain a lot of water, and should also be precooked so they don't weigh down your pizza.

PIZZA NIGHT PREP

The key to any successful wood-fired oven cooking session is time management and attention to detail. Set aside the proper amount of time to organize and prepare, and you will be rewarded with a pizza party that flows naturally. Not only will you supply quality entertainment for your guests, but also, more importantly, there will be plenty of delicious food and drink and it will seem effortless.

While it is not necessary to make your pizza dough the day before you plan to use it, I highly recommend it. The dough develops more character when left to rise overnight in the refrigerator. In addition, it is one less task you need to perform on the day of the festivities.

I like to do all my shopping the day before I plan to prepare the ingredients, since I inevitably forget something and can use the extra time to get what slipped through the cracks. Likewise, thoughtful guests often suggest bringing something to contribute to the dinner—a perfect chance for them to do the final round of shopping for you.

Once the shopping is out of the way and the dough is busy doing its thing, I take time to straighten up the area around the oven where guests will congregate. In the morning I stack the choicest wood and kindling close to the hearth and build my starter fire in the mouth of the oven. I will return later to ignite it while I set up the pizza prep table. In the afternoon I begin to organize the tools I'll need for the evening: peels, fire poker, wire brush/broom, and fire extinguisher.

Roughly two to two and a half hours before guests are scheduled to arrive, I light the fire and start to prep all the ingredients for the night. I revisit the dough and portion it into individual pizzas in time for its final rise, make a quick no-cook tomato sauce, and even test that night's cocktail or beverage offering to make sure it is what I had in mind.

Then final touches take shape: setting the table, polishing glasses, cutting flowers and herbs from the yard for the table and the pizzas alike. When everything is sewn up tight, I take a moment to relax and admire the fire I have built, choose some appropriate music, and light a few candles around the courtyard. The first guests begin to trickle in . . . and so it begins.

Find a nice table that doubles as a workspace. This is where you'll assemble pizzas, refill wine glasses, and discuss the menu. Arrange your ingredients in an appetizing display and be prepared for your guests to eat with their eyes.

WHAT TO DRINK

When it comes to drinking and dining, the choices you make falls under the umbrella of "drink what you think." I go to great lengths to curate food and beverage pairings for my guests, but that's because I find it wildly entertaining. However, you need not obsess over what goes with what; pretension is not an element of cooking with a wood-fired oven.

When I go out for pizza in Italy, usually Sunday evenings after the final soccer matches have been played, I drink what I see everyone else drinking: beer. Particularly, *birra alla spina*, an ice-cold pint of lager drawn from the tap. Italians believe carbonation aids in digesting flour, and who can argue? Pizza and beer are a seamless combination.

Think beer is too blue-collar for your upscale pies? Opt for an imported brand or a craft brew in a minikeg. You will get the "on tap" vibe and around ten pints' worth.

Cocktails have their place as well when you are cooking out of the wood oven. I like bright, refreshing drinks that can be premeasured, served over ice. You need to be busy tending the fire, not tending the bar.

Wine is a fine choice to pair with pizzas as well. The smokiness of the pies and the saltiness of the charcuterie stand up to big reds and crisp whites. I tend to save the better bottles for sit-down dinners; go with a wine you wouldn't mind serving in a tumbler rather than stemware. Make an impression and choose a magnum or two. Big bottles mean big fun, and the wines seem more delicious bottled in this way.

For the reds, Sangiovese is the grape that makes Chianti Classico spectacular, and you can be drinking very well for around $20 a bottle. Gamay is a French varietal that is the backbone of Cru Beaujolais, and accompanies pizza very well. It's light but structured, and a far cry from the candy-like Beaujolais nouveau. A real treat if you can find it is Lambrusco, a slightly sweet, lightly effervescent red wine from central Italy. It's inexpensive and meant to be consumed young, and its low alcohol content makes it ideal for daytime pizza parties. Avoid the eponymous Riunite brand—On ice? Not nice.

If I had to choose a white wine to drink with pizza I would choose a pink one—rosé. Kidding aside, rosé is an ideal palate cleanser for some of the big flavors that emerge from the oven: garlic, sausage, clams, tomatoes, mushrooms. Rosé works with them all. Opt for a balanced bottle that has both dry and fruit notes, or even bubbles.

Finally, let's talk cocktails. The negroni is a party favorite and an excellent match with pizza, made of equal parts gin, sweet vermouth, and Campari. Simply mix a small batch and transfer to an attractive pitcher so guests can help themselves. I recommend using a high-quality gin such as Hendrick's or St. George Botanivore. Don't forget to provide ice and fresh orange peel for garnish.

NEGRONI

Makes 1 Drink

2 ounces ice
1 ounce high quality gin such as Hendrick's or
  St. George Botanivore
1 ounce sweet vermouth such as Dolin
1 ounce Campari, or substitute Aperol
Fresh orange peel pieces, about 1 inch wide
  and 3 inches long

PIZZA NIGHT TIMELINE

1. The day before the event, make the pizza dough and refrigerate it overnight. Create a menu and shop for the toppings, side dishes, and any other food you will need. Don't forget the drinks.

2. The morning of the party, tidy up the oven area, stack wood, gather tools, and build the starter fire (but don't light it yet).

3. Two to two and a half hours before guests arrive, light the fire and prep the toppings and sauces. Set up the work area where you'll fashion the pies and sides.

4. Portion the dough for the final rise. Move the fire, then feed it. Clean and clear the oven floor.

5. Precook in the oven any ingredients that need extra time.

6. Set the table and set the mood.

Seasonal Salads

When you've had your fill of pizza and you'd like just a bit of something fresh to counter the smoky, charred delights you have enjoyed, choose a salad. I prefer to serve a few side salads throughout the evening, to be eaten before or after the pizza. I even like to pair a lightly dressed leafy arugula and mint salad with individual calzones for an all-in-one entrée.

Try to have at least one salad ready about the time guests arrive. If you are running a little behind in prep or the dough needs a while longer to proof, you will have something delicious to offer the hungry. If you can, avoid leaving your guests standing around waiting to be fed or, worse yet, drinking on an empty stomach. See Chapter 9 for a few stellar seasonal salad recipes.

MENU IDEAS

A wood-fired pizza oven gathering is an occasion that takes a bit of forethought. Yes, there is a lot of preparation, but before that, decisions must be made about what to serve.

I always take into consideration the dietary restrictions or allergies of my guests; no one wants to be handed bland choices or second-thought alternatives. Offer anyone with special needs a variation on the existing menu so they feel included, or tweak it slightly, showcasing a special ingredient you added solely for them.

Maybe it's because I spent so many years in restaurant kitchens, where there are razor-thin profit margins, but I try building at least a portion of my menu based on items I already have on hand. A pizza session is a fantastic way to clean out your refrigerator: Odd bits of charcuterie and cheeses, lone vegetables, or those last few olives rolling around the jar can combine to create a house specialty!

Here are a few themed menus to get you started. Mix and match if you like. And try to keep it seasonal and local; the produce tastes better when it wasn't flown in from halfway around the globe.

High and dry. The extremely high temperature and intensely dry conditions of a wood-fired pizza oven combine to provide a uniquely concentrated and rapid baking experience. Watch the dough blister and the toppings sizzle next to the roiling flames.

A WOOD-FIRED SUMMER SOLSTICE

The longest day of the year deserves a leisurely, prolonged dinner party. Squeeze in an extra course and toast the setting sun.

WARM MONTRACHET
WRAPPED IN GRAPE LEAVES
with ROASTED WINE GRAPES
and FLATBREAD
(PAGE 194)

FARM STAND
VEGETABLE SALAD
(PAGE 218)

QUATTRO STAGIONI
(FOUR SEASONS PIZZA)
(PAGE 93)

SWEET HAND PIE
OF ROASTED STONE FRUITS
and FRANGIPANE
(PAGE 184)

CELEBRATING THE ARRIVAL OF SPRINGTIME

The weather has finally turned for the better. Celebrate at the first sign of organic asparagus in the market.

MOREL MUSHROOM
PIZZA with CREAM and
A SUNNY-SIDE UP EGG
(PAGE 160)

EGGPLANT ROASTED
IN THE COALS
(PAGE 198)

CRACKED LOBSTERS ROASTED
with PAPRIKA BUTTER
(PAGE 204)

SWEET HAND PIE OF
ROASTED CHERRIES with
GRAPPA and AMARETTI
(PAGE 186)

WHEN FAMILY VISITS

You want to spend quality time with the family while they are visiting, not the entire day cooking. Still, everyone needs to eat. Defrost the extra dough you made and light a fire.

MERGUEZ FLATBREAD with
ZUCCHINI, SMOKY EGGPLANT,
and CILANTRO
(PAGE 109)

SHAKSHUKA (BAKED EGGS
with TOMATOES and DUKKA)
(PAGE 202)

LONG-COOKED "POT O' BEANS"
with OKRA, TOMATOES,
and PEPPERS
(PAGE 200)

ROSEMARY FOCACCIA
(PAGE 62)

A HOLIDAY GATHERING

The holiday season is a great opportunity to reconnect with friends you may not have seen during the year. Toss a few simple pizzas for them while you ring in the cheer.

ESCAROLE, PERSIMMON,
and POMEGRANATE SALAD
with TOASTED WALNUT
VINAIGRETTE
(PAGE 215)

BLACK TRUFFLE
and FONTINA PIZZA
(PAGE 164)

SWEET HAND PIE
OF PUMPKIN, WARM SPICES,
and MASCARPONE
(PAGE 182)

AN INTIMATE DINNER FOR TWO

*A menu designed for a special occasion—or if the
special occasion is simply two for dinner.*

GRATIN OF
WILD MUSHROOM CRÈPES

(PAGE 196)

RIB-EYE STEAK GRILLED
"IN THE WINDOW"
with SALSA VERDE

(PAGE 212)

ROASTED WINTER
VEGETABLES IN DUCK FAT
and ROSEMARY

(PAGE 199)

OVEN-ROASTED
FRUITS

(PAGE 213)

PIZZA ON A SCHOOL NIGHT

*In my house there is no debate—pepperoni pizza
is what the boy wants. Make it a special school night.*

SIMPLE ARUGULA
and HERB SALAD

(PAGE 217)

NUMBER ONE
PEPPERONI PIZZA

(PAGE 85)

OVEN-ROASTED
FRUITS

(PAGE 213)

PART TWO
THE RECIPES

3 THE DOUGH

ALL GREAT *PIZZAIOLI* have their tried and true dough recipes. Through years of trial and error, I've developed a variety of easily executable and versatile dough recipes that will be the foundation for your entire wood-fired pizza oven experience. These recipes range from fundamental to complex in flavor, yet almost all can be made using basic ingredients found in a well-stocked supermarket. Still, a few are made livelier by the addition of a handful of specialty components.

The techniques for building these doughs are straightforward and generally the same throughout, yet the recipes yield different results, according to the flavors of the ingredients. Once you've learned how to make great pizza dough at home, you will be well on your way to maximizing the potential of your wood-fired oven.

BASIC GO-TO EASY PIZZA DOUGH

MAKES EIGHT TO TEN 10-INCH PIZZAS
Prep time: 2 hours, plus up to 24 hours to rise

This recipe is a great introduction to creating fresh, hand-tossed pizzas at home. Start with these basic building blocks and techniques for a versatile dough, and you will fall in love all over again with the world's most perfect food. Whenever possible, go with organic flour and always use the highest quality olive oil your budget will allow. Always use all-natural active dry yeast, such as Fleischmann's brand, and check that it is well before its expiration date. If the yeast isn't alive and kicking, your pizzas won't be either. This dough transforms into a living, breathing, edible entity, and is a textbook example of the sum being greater than its parts. Start this recipe a full 24 hours before baking and allow it to develop a more complex flavor as it refrigerates overnight.

FOR THE SPONGE
1 cup plus 2 tablespoons lukewarm water
1 tablespoon active dry yeast
4½ ounces (1 cup) all-purpose flour

FOR THE DOUGH
1¾ pounds (6½ cups) all-purpose flour
2 tablespoons kosher salt
1½ cups cold water
½ cup extra-virgin olive oil

TO MAKE THE SPONGE

1. Put the warm water in the work bowl of a stand mixer and sprinkle the yeast evenly over the surface. Briefly stir to moisten all the yeast. Add the flour and whisk until no lumps are visible and the entire mixture is moistened. Set the bowl in a warm location.

2. After 30 to 40 minutes, you should notice small bubbles beginning to form on the surface of the sponge and a pleasant "bready-yeasty" smell beginning to arise. If after 40 minutes the sponge does not seem active, wait another 15 minutes and check again. If it still does not seem bubbly and aromatic, discard the sponge and start over, making sure that the water you use is warm to the touch but not scalding and that your yeast is not expired. →

TO MAKE THE DOUGH

1. In a large bowl, combine the flour and salt and mix well. Transfer 1½ cups of the flour-salt mixture to the bubbly sponge and add the cold water. Whisk thoroughly and let sit for another 30 minutes.

2. Attach the dough hook to your mixer. Add the remaining flour mixture and the olive oil to the work bowl and knead on medium-low speed for 3 to 5 minutes. Stop the mixer once midway through and push the forming dough off the hook to ensure even kneading. The dough should begin to clean the sides of the bowl, becoming slightly sticky and elastic.

3. Gather up the moist, soft dough ball and transfer it to a large bowl to be left to proof. (If the dough seems too dry, knead it a few times by hand with a few drops of water. If it seems too wet and difficult to handle, sprinkle it with some flour and knead gently to make a manageable dough ball that maintains a slight shape.)

4. Leave the dough in the bowl, cover with plastic wrap or a kitchen towel, and leave in a warm place for about 2 hours. The dough should nearly double in size and become noticeably aromatic. If time allows, the dough will benefit from a long, steady rise in the refrigerator—overnight is best, or even up to 2 days. The flavor will be more complex and the dough will become more pliant with this protracted fermentation process.

5. Either proceed now or, on the following day, punch down the dough by kneading it a few turns on a lightly floured work surface, then divide it into 8 to 10 equal portions, roughly 8 ounces each. Form the dough balls into small pillows by making a circular motion with both cupped hands on a lightly floured work surface. Press and gently turn each pillow to create a seamless round dough ball. (At this point the dough can be wrapped in plastic and frozen for up to a month, then allowed to thaw slowly in the refrigerator before proceeding with the following step.)

6. Arrange the dough balls on a floured tray about 3 inches apart and cover loosely with plastic wrap. Set aside at room temperature to proof for an additional 1 hour. Notice the transformation from dense, cool dough to airy pillows and an increase in the overall size as the dough puffs. You are now ready to shape the dough for pizzas.

A CLOSER LOOK: *"Proof" is a term bakers use to describe the leavening of the dough as the yeast begins the fermentation process and creates carbon dioxide. Those crispy burned bubbles on the pizza crust we love? That is a sign of properly fermented dough.*

HOW TO SHAPE A PIZZA

Once you have your dough proofed, your ingredients selected, and your oven hot and ready, these simple instructions will give your pizzas the perfect shape.

Place a wooden peel on a clean surface and dust it with flour. Gather the proofed dough and sprinkle both sides with flour.

Use your fingertips to begin flattening the pizza into a wide circle about 1-inch thick.

Pick up the dough and begin pinching and flattening between your thumb and forefingers, rotating as you go, to create a border.

Place your fists under the dough and stretch it under its own weight. Give the dough a toss if you'd like! This iconic technique creates centrifugal force and expands the dough in a circular shape.

Place the dough back on the pizza peel. Smooth out any thick spots with your fingertips and create a general circular shape and accentuate the crust.

The dough should have an even thickness throughout and measure approximately 10-inches in diameter.

ELEVATED PIZZA DOUGH

MAKES EIGHT TO TEN 10-INCH PIZZAS
Prep time: 2 hours, plus up to 24 hours to rise

While the method for making this dough is the same as in the basic recipe, it is elevated to new heights by the simple addition of rye flour (I like Bob's Red Mill brand). Substituting rye flour for wheat in the sponge creates a deeply flavored, nutty, and somewhat sour starter. Rye flour doesn't provide much in the way of gluten, but that will be made up in the body of the dough. You likely won't find rye flour in pizza dough anywhere but in the northern regions of Italy, where the grain was traditionally harvested. Consequently, it pairs nicely with pizzas featuring game and cured meats, staples of the northern table.

FOR THE SPONGE

1 cup plus 2 tablespoons lukewarm water
1 tablespoon active dry yeast
4½ ounces (1 cup) rye flour

FOR THE DOUGH

13½ ounces (3 cups) 00 flour
12 ounces (2¾ cups) all-purpose flour
2 tablespoons kosher salt
1½ cups cold water
½ cup extra-virgin olive oil

TO MAKE THE SPONGE

1. Put the warm water in the work bowl of a stand mixer and sprinkle the yeast evenly over the surface. Briefly stir to moisten all the yeast. Add the rye flour and whisk until no lumps are visible and the entire mixture is moistened. Set the bowl in a warm location.

2. After 30 to 40 minutes, you should notice small bubbles beginning to form on the surface of the sponge and a pleasant "bready-yeasty" smell beginning to arise. If after 40 minutes the sponge does not seem active, wait another 15 minutes and check again. If it still does not seem bubbly and aromatic, discard the sponge and start over, making sure that the water you use is warm to the touch but not scalding and that your yeast is not expired.

TO MAKE THE DOUGH

1. In a large bowl, combine the two wheat flours and salt and mix well. Transfer 1½ cups of the flour-salt mixture to the bubbly sponge and add the cold water. Whisk thoroughly and let sit for another 30 minutes.

2. Attach the dough hook to your mixer. Add the remaining flour mixture and the olive oil to the work bowl and knead on medium-low speed for 3 to 5 minutes. Stop the mixer once midway through and push the forming dough off the hook to ensure even kneading. The dough should begin to clean the sides of the bowl, becoming slightly sticky and elastic.

3. Gather up the moist, soft dough ball and transfer it to a large bowl to be left to proof. (If the dough seems too dry, knead it a few times by hand with a few drops of water. If it seems too wet and difficult to handle, sprinkle it with some flour and knead gently to make a manageable dough ball that maintains a slight shape.)

4. Leave the dough in the bowl, cover with plastic wrap or a kitchen towel, and leave in a warm place for about 2 hours. The dough should nearly double in size and become noticeably aromatic. If time allows, the dough will benefit from a long, steady rise in the refrigerator—overnight is best, or even up to 2 days. The flavor will be more complex and the dough will become more pliant with this protracted fermentation process.

5. Either proceed now or, on the following day, punch down the dough by kneading it a few turns on a lightly floured work surface, then divide it into 8 to 10 equal portions, roughly 8 ounces each. Form the dough balls into small pillows by making a circular motion with both cupped hands on a lightly floured work surface. Press and gently turn each pillow to create a seamless round dough ball. (At this point the dough can be wrapped in plastic and frozen for up to a month, then allowed to thaw slowly in the refrigerator before proceeding with the following step.)

6. Arrange the dough balls on a floured tray about 3 inches apart and cover loosely with plastic wrap. Set aside at room temperature to proof for an additional 1 hour. Notice the transformation from dense, cool dough to airy pillows and an increase in the overall size as the dough puffs. You are now ready to shape the dough for pizzas.

A CLOSER LOOK: *I like to keep my unused rye flour in the freezer to maintain freshness, since I don't use it very often between pizza sessions. The 00 wheat flour never seems to stay stocked in my house, so I'm less concerned with freshness. I use it constantly when making fresh pastas, desserts, and of course wood oven–baked pizzas.*

SPELT PIZZA DOUGH

**MAKES TWO 10-INCH OR
THREE 8-INCH PIZZAS**
Prep time: 2 hours, plus up to 24 hours to rise

Spelt flour (Bob's Red Mill is one brand I like) is a hybrid of the common wheat flour known all over Italy as emmer or farro. Some accounts date the grain to 7,000 BCE, which makes it one of humanity's most ancient grains. This dough is built using a spelt starter for the sponge, and has a small addition of semolina to add another dimension to the texture. Spelt is easily digestible thanks to its high water solubility, which makes it an ideal grain for those who have difficulty digesting wheat flour.

FOR THE SPONGE

¼ cup plus 2 tablespoons lukewarm water

1 teaspoon active dry yeast

2 ounces (¼ cup plus 3 tablespoons) spelt flour

FOR THE DOUGH

4½ ounces (1 cup) all-purpose flour

2 ounces (¼ cup plus 3 tablespoons) semolina flour

1 tablespoon kosher salt

½ cup cold water

2 tablespoons extra-virgin olive oil

TO MAKE THE SPONGE

1. Put the warm water in the work bowl of a stand mixer and sprinkle the yeast evenly over the surface. Briefly stir to moisten all the yeast. Add the spelt flour and whisk until no lumps are visible and the entire mixture is moistened. Set the bowl in a warm location.

2. After 30 to 40 minutes, you should notice small bubbles beginning to form on the surface of the sponge and a pleasant "bready-yeasty" smell beginning to arise. If after 40 minutes the sponge does not seem active, wait another 15 minutes and check again. If it still does not seem bubbly and aromatic, discard the sponge and start over, making sure that the water you use is warm to the touch but not scalding and that your yeast is not expired.

1. In a large bowl, combine the all-purpose flour, semolina flour, and salt and mix well. Transfer ½ cup of the flour-salt mixture to the bubbly sponge and add the cold water. Whisk thoroughly and let sit for another 30 minutes.

2. Attach the dough hook to your mixer. Add the remaining flour mixture and the olive oil to the work bowl and knead on medium-low speed for 3 to 5 minutes. Stop the mixer once midway through and push the forming dough off the hook to ensure even kneading. The dough should begin to clean the sides of the bowl, becoming slightly sticky and elastic.

3. Gather up the moist, soft dough ball and transfer it to a large bowl to be left to proof. (If the dough seems too dry, knead it a few times by hand with a few drops of water. If it seems too wet and difficult to handle, sprinkle it with some flour and knead gently to make a manageable dough ball that maintains a slight shape.)

4. Leave the dough in the bowl, cover with plastic wrap or a kitchen towel, and leave in a warm place for about 2 hours. The dough should nearly double in size and become noticeably aromatic. If time allows, the dough will benefit from a long, steady rise in the refrigerator—overnight is best, or even up to 2 days. The flavor will be more complex and the dough will become more pliant with this protracted fermentation process.

5. Either proceed now or, on the following day, punch down the dough by kneading it a few turns on a lightly floured work surface, then divide it into 2 or 3 equal portions. Form the dough balls into small pillows by making a circular motion with both cupped hands on a lightly floured work surface. Press and gently turn each pillow to create a seamless round dough ball. (At this point the dough can be wrapped in plastic and frozen for up to a month, then allowed to thaw slowly in the refrigerator before proceeding with the following step.)

6. Arrange the dough balls on a floured tray about 3 inches apart and cover loosely with plastic wrap. Set aside at room temperature to proof for an additional 1 hour. Notice the transformation from dense, cool dough to airy pillows and an increase in the overall size as the dough puffs. You are now ready to shape the dough for pizzas.

WHOLE-WHEAT PIZZA DOUGH

MAKES THREE 8-INCH PIZZAS

Prep time: 2 hours, plus up to 24 hours to rise

This is a variation on the previous dough recipes for those who want to get a bit more whole grain in their diet. The addition of a small amount of whole-wheat flour imparts a pleasant nuttiness to the final product and pairs nicely with a variety of ingredients. If you cannot find 00 flour, go ahead and use all-purpose flour in its place. I suggest making slightly smaller 8-inch pizzas; due to the nature of the wheat you'll get a softer, slightly chewy pie.

FOR THE SPONGE

¼ cup plus 2 tablespoons lukewarm water

1 teaspoon active dry yeast

2 ounces (¼ cup plus 3 tablespoons) 00 flour

FOR THE DOUGH

9 ounces (2 cups) all-purpose flour

2¾ ounces (½ cup plus 2 tablespoons) whole-wheat flour

1 tablespoon plus 1 teaspoon kosher salt

½ cup cold water

2 tablespoons extra-virgin olive oil

TO MAKE THE SPONGE

1. Put the warm water in the work bowl of a stand mixer and sprinkle the yeast evenly over the surface. Briefly stir to moisten all the yeast. Add the 00 flour and whisk until no lumps are visible and the entire mixture is moistened. Set the bowl in a warm location.

2. After 30 to 40 minutes, you should notice small bubbles beginning to form on the surface of the sponge and a pleasant "bready-yeasty" smell beginning to arise. If after 40 minutes the sponge does not seem active, wait another 15 minutes and check again. If it still does not seem bubbly and aromatic, discard the sponge and start over, making sure that the water you use is warm to the touch but not scalding and that your yeast is not expired.

TO MAKE THE DOUGH

1. In a large bowl, combine the all-purpose and whole-wheat flours and salt and mix well. Transfer ½ cup of the flour-salt mixture to the bubbly sponge and add the cold water. Whisk thoroughly and let sit for another 30 minutes.

2. Attach the dough hook to your mixer. Add the remaining flour mixture and the olive oil to the work bowl and knead on medium-low speed for 3 to

5 minutes. Stop the mixer once midway through and push the forming dough off the hook to ensure even kneading. The dough should begin to clean the sides of the bowl, becoming slightly sticky and elastic.

3. Gather up the moist, soft dough ball and transfer it to a large bowl to be left to proof. (If the dough seems too dry, knead it a few times by hand with a few drops of water. If it seems too wet and difficult to handle, sprinkle it with some flour and knead gently to make a manageable dough ball that maintains a slight shape.)

4. Leave the dough in the bowl, cover with plastic wrap or a kitchen towel, and leave in a warm place for about 2 hours. The dough should nearly double in size and become noticeably aromatic. If time allows, the dough will benefit from a long, steady rise in the refrigerator—overnight is best, or even up to 2 days. The flavor will be more complex and the dough will become more pliant with this protracted fermentation process.

5. Either proceed now or, on the following day, punch down the dough by kneading it a few turns on a lightly floured work surface, then divide it into 3 equal portions, roughly 6 ounces each. Form the dough balls into small pillows by making a circular motion with both cupped hands on a lightly floured work surface. Press and gently turn each pillow to create a seamless round dough ball. (At this point the dough can be wrapped in plastic and frozen for up to a month, then allowed to thaw slowly in the refrigerator before proceeding with the following step.)

6. Arrange the dough balls on a floured tray about 3 inches apart and cover loosely with plastic wrap. Set aside at room temperature to proof for an additional 1 hour. Notice the transformation from dense, cool dough to airy pillows and an increase in the overall size as the dough puffs. You are now ready to shape the dough for pizzas.

WHAT TO DRINK: *I like hearty red wines from the Rhône region to stand up to the complex flavors of the whole-wheat dough.*

GLUTEN-FREE PIZZA DOUGH

MAKES TWO 9-BY-13-INCH PIZZAS
Prep time: 2 hours, plus up to 24 hours to rise
Cook time: 10 to 20 minutes

There are several brands of gluten-free flour on the market now. I prefer the well-tested Cup4Cup flour. It is a straight one-for-one substitute for normal flour and contains a number of hard-to-find ingredients that have been blended together for your convenience. This flour is readily available at Whole Foods Market or online, and conveniently sold in 3-pound bags—enough for several pizza sessions. I recommend that you use this dough as soon as possible after putting it together as it does not store well.

FOR THE SPONGE

1 cup lukewarm water

¼ cup whole milk, at room temperature

1 tablespoon plus 2 teaspoons active dry yeast

1 extra-large egg

FOR THE DOUGH

1½ pounds (5¼ cups) gluten-free flour

2 teaspoons baking powder, sifted

2 teaspoons kosher salt

2 teaspoons sugar

2 tablespoons extra-virgin olive oil, divided

TO MAKE THE SPONGE

1. In a small bowl, combine the warm water and milk. Sprinkle the yeast evenly over the surface and stir to combine. Set aside in a warm spot until active and bubbly, about 15 minutes.

2. When the yeast mixture is active and bubbly, lightly whisk in the egg.

TO MAKE THE DOUGH

1. Attach the paddle to your stand mixer. In the work bowl, combine the flour, baking powder, salt, and sugar and mix on low speed.

2. Add the bubbly sponge to the work bowl and mix on low speed until combined, 2 to 3 minutes.

3. Gather the dough and transfer to an unfloured work surface. Briefly knead the dough to combine, 4 or 5 turns total.

4. Divide the dough into two equal portions and wrap each tightly in plastic wrap. Gently shape each into a 2-inch-thick disc. Allow to rise in a warm spot for 45 minutes.

5. Preheat the wood oven to approximately 500°F. Brush a quarter sheet pan with 1 tablespoon of the olive oil.

6. Using a wooden rolling pin, roll out the dough on a clean, dry, unfloured surface to ¼-inch thickness, and transfer to the prepared sheet pan. With a sharp paring knife, trim away any excess dough that hangs over the sides of the tray. Fill in any gaps by using the trimmed pieces, pressing the seams together. The entire tray should be filled to the edges. With the tines of a fork, prick the entire surface of the dough.

7. Brush the remaining 1 tablespoon of olive oil over the top of the dough. Transfer to a warm spot and allow the dough to proof for 15 minutes before baking.

8. Bake the dough in a relatively cool zone of the oven, away from the fire, until lightly browned, 8 to 10 minutes, making sure to rotate frequently. Remove the tray from the oven and allow to cool slightly. Add the toppings of your choice and return to the hot oven and bake until warmed through, about 5 minutes more.

NORTH AFRICAN FLATBREAD

MAKES TWO FLATBREADS

Prep time: 2½ hours

Cook time: 2 to 3 minutes per flatbread

I suggest using a blend of two different flours for this simple recipe. Seek out a 100 percent whole-grain flour, such as Community Grains hard red winter wheat, for the body of the dough, and semolina flour for added texture. This is an exciting time to be baking, because the quest for understanding our digestive processes and the rise of gluten intolerance have pushed independent flour mills—and, by association, farmers—to explore alternative grains. How the grain is milled has become an important factor in turning back the clock to a more nutritious and healthy style of vitamin intake through whole grains.

FOR THE SPONGE

⅔ cup lukewarm water

½ teaspoon active dry yeast

1 tablespoon extra-virgin olive oil, plus more for topping

FOR THE DOUGH

6 ounces (1¼ cups plus 2 tablespoons) 100% whole-grain flour

1½ ounces (¼ cup) semolina flour

½ teaspoon kosher salt

3 tablespoons za'atar (optional; see A Closer Look)

TO MAKE THE SPONGE

1. Put the warm water in the work bowl of a stand mixer and sprinkle the yeast evenly over the surface. Stir to dissolve. Add the olive oil and mix by hand. Set the work bowl in a warm location.

2. After 20 to 30 minutes, you should notice small bubbles beginning to form on the surface of the sponge and a pleasant "bready-yeasty" smell beginning to arise.

TO MAKE THE DOUGH

1. In a large bowl, combine the whole-grain and semolina flours and the salt. Add the flour mixture to the bubbly sponge all at once.

2. Attach the dough hook to your mixer. Mix on medium-low speed until a soft, slightly sticky dough forms and pulls away from the side of the bowl. Continue mixing for 3 minutes. If the dough appears too wet, add another tablespoon of whole-grain flour. If it appears too dry and has a "shaggy" appearance, add 1 teaspoon water. Mix until no lumps appear and you have a smooth dough, about another minute.

3. Transfer the dough to a medium bowl, cover with plastic wrap, and allow to rise in a warm place until roughly doubled in size, 1 to 2 hours.

4. When the dough has risen, uncover and punch it down. Turn it out onto a lightly floured work surface and knead two or three times. Divide the dough into two equal portions.

5. Using a rolling pin or pasta machine, roll the dough very thinly and evenly to about ⅛-inch thickness. Transfer to a lightly floured peel, brush with olive oil, and scatter the za'atar evenly over the surface (if using). Gently press the spice into the dough using your fingertips.

6. Bake directly on the floor of your medium-hot wood-fired oven until blistered and colored but not totally crisp, 2 to 3 minutes. Enjoy immediately.

A CLOSER LOOK: *Za'atar is a Middle Eastern spice blend. With its deep herbal flavor, it is a natural complement to many of the dishes cooked in the wood oven. A blend of dried thyme, oregano, and marjoram, this trinity is often mixed with salt and ground sumac berries. I like the version that contains sesame seeds, either black or white, for added nuttiness. If you can't find za'atar where you shop, create an impromptu version using some or all of the aforementioned dried herbs. Season with salt, sesame seeds, and sumac, if you like.*

ROSEMARY FOCACCIA

MAKES ONE 12-BY-16-INCH FOCACCIA

Prep time: 2 hours
Cook time: 20 to 30 minutes

Focaccia, the early ancestor of pizza, is popular all over Italy but has lost its way in the United States. Examples found stateside range from soggy and dry (hard to achieve both at once!), to overburdened with toppings. Fortunately, this rendition restores Old World glory with the addition of semolina and a bake directly on the oven floor. In my opinion, the afternoon is the ideal time to enjoy a wedge of focaccia, paired expertly with an aperitivo or a flute of prosecco. A variety of toppings work well on focaccia, but simpler is better for this dough. Fresh rosemary, extra-virgin olive oil, and crunchy salt (I like Maldon sea salt flakes) are all that's really required. I like to cut my focaccia into large wedges or rectangular "fingers" that I can wrap in a napkin and pass to my guests so they can enjoy a drink in one hand and a salty snack in the other.

FOR THE SPONGE

1½ cups lukewarm water

2 tablespoons plus 2 teaspoons active dry yeast

½ cup extra-virgin olive oil

FOR THE DOUGH

16 ounces (3½ cups) bread flour

9¼ ounces (2 cups) semolina flour

1 tablespoon kosher salt

¼ cup extra-virgin olive oil

½ cup fresh rosemary leaves

2 tablespoons sea salt flakes

TO MAKE THE SPONGE

1. Put the warm water in the work bowl of a stand mixer and sprinkle the yeast evenly over the surface. Stir to dissolve. Add the olive oil and mix by hand. Set the work bowl in a warm location.

2. After 20 to 30 minutes, you should notice small bubbles beginning to form on the surface of the sponge and a pleasant "bready-yeasty" smell beginning to arise.

TO MAKE THE DOUGH

1. Line a half sheet pan with parchment paper.

2. In a large bowl, combine the bread and semolina flours and the salt.

3. Attach the dough hook to your mixer. Mix the sponge on medium-low speed. Gradually add the flour mixture, a cup at a time, allowing the flours to be absorbed into the wet mixture before adding more. Mix thoroughly for 5 minutes, making sure no dry ingredients remain.

4. Using a spatula, scrape out the dough directly onto the prepared sheet pan and gently spread out the dough. Don't worry if it doesn't fully cover the parchment. Allow the dough to rest, uncovered, in a warm spot for 20 minutes.

5. Using your fingers, spread the dough a bit more evenly into the pan, trying to take the dough all the way to the edges. Allow the dough to rest for another 20 minutes and then repeat until the entire sheet tray is covered evenly with the focaccia dough. Allow to rest a final time until the dough has risen and filled the sheet tray completely, another 20 to 30 minutes.

6. You are now ready to top the focaccia. Dip your fingertips in the olive oil and press them into the dough to make shallow dimples all over the surface. Repeat until the entire sheet pan is pockmarked and oily.

7. Mix the rosemary with the remaining olive oil. Dot the surface with the herbs, pressing them gently into the dough, and drizzle any remaining oil over the focaccia. Scatter the salt flakes evenly over the surface. The focaccia is now ready for the oven.

TO BAKE THE FOCACCIA

1. In your wood-fired oven, allow a medium-hot fire to burn down so it is no longer flaming. You should have a nice mass of glowing embers and a fully heated oven. If you have a laser thermometer, you are looking for a floor temperature of around 425°F.

2. Insert the sheet tray opposite the fire source and bake until the focaccia is puffed and deep golden. I like to rotate the pan frequently; this allows me to check the progress of the bake and also gauge the fire's intensity. If it's too cool, I add a small piece of wood; too hot and I can cover the dough loosely with a piece of heavy aluminum foil to slow the browning on the surface.

3. Approximately 20 minutes of baking should set the dough but, depending on your fire, it may take another 10 minutes. Remove the pan from the oven and allow it to cool slightly.

4. With a sharp knife, cut around the edges of the dough and release it from the pan in one slab. The parchment paper should still be on the baked focaccia, but if it isn't, don't fret.

5. Slide the dough back onto the warm oven floor for a final bake. This ensures a nice, evenly crispy crust.

6. Transfer to a cooling rack. When cool, invert and peel off the parchment paper. Cut into rectangular "fingers" and serve.

SWEET DOUGH FOR HAND PIES

MAKES TWO 6-INCH PIES
Prep time: 30 to 40 minutes

This is a variation of the all-purpose dough the legendary Jacques Pépin taught the pastry department at Chez Panisse. He was generous enough to share his technique with us young cooks, and it has become the de facto sweet dough for a legion of pastry chefs since. While it has a variety of applications, both sweet and savory, I like to use it in the wood oven to make small "hand pies" filled with a variety of sweet fillings. Cook them slowly in the window of the hearth so the sugar caramelizes and the pastry crisps and browns.

4½ ounces (1 cup) all-purpose flour

4½ ounces (1 cup) 00 flour

1 teaspoon sugar

¼ teaspoon kosher salt

¾ cup (1½ sticks) very cold unsalted butter, cut into 12 equal cubes, divided

½ cup ice water

1. In the bowl of a stand mixer fitted with the paddle attachment, mix the two flours, sugar, and salt just to combine.

2. Add 8 of the butter cubes and mix on low speed until the butter begins to break down and the mixture has a sandy appearance. Stop the mixer and sort through the unformed dough by hand, using your fingers to pinch together any large chunks of butter that remain. Mix on low for 2 or 4 more turns. Add the remaining 4 butter cubes and again mix on low until the butter is slightly incorporated, about 2 minutes. Stop the mixer and remove the work bowl. Repeat the pinching step and make sure there are no remaining large chunks of butter in the mixture.

3. Make a well in the center of the shaggy mass. Add the ice water to the well and gently cover the water pool with the surrounding dough crumbs. Let the dough stand for 5 minutes to allow it to absorb some of the water.

4. Mix the dough by hand, quickly and evenly. Knead the dough only long enough so it forms a moist, slightly sticky ball, being careful not to overwork it.

5. Divide the dough into two equal portions and wrap each in plastic wrap. Flatten each ball into a smooth disc about ½ inch thick. The dough should have a nice, even marbled appearance, streaked with butter.

6. Refrigerate the dough until ready to use, at least 2 hours and up to 24 hours.

PREP TIP: *Making the dough the day before you intend to use it allows it to properly hydrate and rest. Or you can freeze the plastic-wrapped discs for up to 2 months. Defrost in the refrigerator overnight.*

4 SAUCES AND CONDIMENTS

ONE OF THE ESSENTIAL BUILDING BLOCKS of a delicious pizza is, of course, a well-made and complementary sauce. Artful pizza makers realize it is a delicate balance, so don't over-sauce! A properly sauced pie maintains a crisp crust, prohibits the cheese from burning, and adds culinary significance. In jazz terms, it's the hardworking rhythm section, the backbeat that keeps the party thumping.

You'll find that some pizzas have components that succeed unadorned; those don't require a sauce at all. A perfectly made condiment, such as a tapenade, drizzled about, is the ideal foil to let those starring elements shine.

I've included sauces that range from a basic marinara to a complexly flavored and nuanced wild fennel condiment, and even a traditional North African spicy paste known as harissa. All have their place on a blistery wood-fired dough. You'll find yourself habitually returning to these classic sauces and condiments, mixing and matching them with all manner of ingredients.

And a quick safety tip: Get into the habit of having all your ingredients at hand, organized for easy access, before you start building your pizza. This will allow you to focus your attention on the pizza in the oven. A distracted *pizzaiolo* is more likely to burn themselves and their pizza.

ESSENTIAL GARLIC OIL

MAKES ABOUT 1½ CUPS
Prep time: 15 minutes

Believe it or not, garlic has a season just like every other vegetable. We're lured into thinking garlic is a year-round staple because of its wide availability, and for the most part it is. But spring is when it reaches its flavorful peak. Spring garlic, or green garlic, as it is also known, has a mild sweetness and a multi-note garlic—not the hot, acrid flavor you encounter when the bulbs have aged. Chopped garlic is extremely volatile; covering it in oil, as in this recipe, prevents oxidation and captures the fresh flavor at the same time.

> 1 bunch spring garlic (4 or 5 shoots), green tops included, or 8 garlic cloves, peeled
> 1 cup extra-virgin olive oil

1. If you are using garlic shoots, peel away the outer layer to reveal the pale inner layer. Slice off the root end and discard, then split the garlic shoots in half lengthwise.

2. Line up the split garlic shoots and slice crosswise into crescents ⅟₁₆ inch thick. Slice the entire white portion and a good deal of the green tops. You should have about ½ cup sliced garlic in total.

3. If you are using garlic cloves, cut them in half and then cut out the bitter germ that runs down the center, and discard it. Slice the cloves thinly, then chop very finely.

4. Transfer the garlic to a small bowl and cover with the oil.

PREP TIP: *For garlic oil that is more homogeneous, transfer the sliced or chopped garlic to a mortar and pestle, add a pinch of salt, and pound, in batches, to a coarse paste. Then add that paste to the oil.*

SIMPLE TOMATO SAUCE

MAKES ABOUT 2 CUPS
Prep time: 5 minutes

1 (28-ounce) can whole peeled tomatoes
¼ cup extra-virgin olive oil
3 or 4 fresh basil leaves
2 teaspoons salt

This is just about the most basic sauce you'll encounter, but it undergoes a transformation in the fiery heat of the wood oven: raw when it goes in and perfectly cooked when it comes out. This hardly amounts to a recipe so much as a procedure. Choose your favorite brand of tomatoes. I like Muir Glen because they are organic and domestic, but imported San Marzanos have a place in my cupboard as well.

1. This could not be simpler. Open the can of tomatoes and add the oil, basil leaves, and salt. Using the wand of an immersion blender, purée until smooth. Or, transfer the ingredients to a countertop blender or food processor and purée until well incorporated.

2. Taste and adjust the seasoning with salt or olive oil.

OVEN-ROASTED RED SAUCE

MAKES ABOUT 2½ CUPS
Prep time: 10 minutes
Cook time: 20 minutes

The best part about firing your wood oven may be the fact that it saves you so much time from washing dirty dishes. Here we scorch a gratin dish layered with basil, onions, and whole ripe tomatoes to add a smoky quality to the finished sauce. Select a gratin dish that can withstand the rigors of the wood oven—high heat, rough treatment—and can snugly hold all the tomatoes in a single layer. When the tomatoes are nicely blistered and have an air of wood smoke about them, simply purée the lot. If you can find organic Early Girl tomatoes, they make a balanced, deep sauce that has good acidity, but Roma tomatoes will serve you well too.

> 2 fresh basil sprigs
> ½ yellow onion, thinly sliced
> 3 pounds ripe organic tomatoes, such as Early Girl or Roma, cored
> ¼ to ½ cup extra-virgin olive oil
> 1 tablespoon salt

1. Line the bottom of the gratin dish with the basil sprigs, followed by the onion slices, and finally the tomatoes, cored-side down. Drizzle the entire dish with the olive oil so the vegetables are well coated, and sprinkle the salt over all.

2. Build a nice hot fire with a generous bed of coals. Place the gratin dish directly next to the active coal bed, as close to the fire as possible, but not in the embers. Select a small piece of wood and add it to the fire to create some extra heat and a bit of smoke as the wood catches.

3. Roast the tomatoes until they are noticeably charred, bubbling, and somewhat collapsed, about 20 minutes. Halfway through, move the dish to the middle of the oven so the tomatoes cook a bit more slowly.

4. Remove the gratin dish and allow it to cool slightly. Transfer the entire contents to a food mill and pass it through. The basil stems, tomato skins, and most of the seeds will be left behind, and you will have a thin purée. If you prefer, return the purée to the gratin dish and reduce further in the oven for a more concentrated sauce.

5. The sauce will keep in an airtight container in the refrigerator for up to 1 week or in the freezer for up to 2 months.

CHARRED SWEET PEPPER AND TOMATO SAUCE

MAKES ABOUT 2 CUPS
Prep time: 25 minutes
Cook time: 20 to 30 minutes

In the late summer, when tomatoes begin to hit their peak and the sweet pepper crop abounds, make a sauce for pizzas (and pastas, too) combining these bright flavors. Roasting the peppers in the wood oven helps make quick work of removing the indigestible skins, while charring the tomatoes accents the natural sugars in the fruit.

3 large red bell peppers, or a mixture of sweet red peppers

2 pounds very ripe organic tomatoes, halved, seeded, and diced

2 teaspoons salt

4 tablespoons extra-virgin olive oil, divided

1 teaspoon smoked paprika

½ teaspoon chili flakes

2 tablespoons unsalted butter, at room temperature

1. Build a very hot fire in the wood oven and allow it to burn down to create an environment in the range of 600° to 700°F.

2. Put the whole peppers in a cast iron skillet and roast in the oven, turning frequently, until the skins are entirely blackened, 10 to 15 minutes. Remove the peppers from the oven, transfer to a bowl, cover with a kitchen towel, and allow to steam for 15 minutes.

3. Meanwhile, line a cazuela with the diced tomatoes, in a 1-inch layer. Season with salt and drizzle with 1 tablespoon of olive oil. Roast in the hottest part of the oven until slightly charred and concentrated, 10 to 15 minutes, stirring occasionally to ensure even colorization. The idea is to expose the surface area of the tomatoes to the intense heat, evaporate the tomato water, and char the flesh. Remove from the oven.

4. When the peppers are cool enough to handle, peel and seed them, reserving the flesh.

5. In a blender or food processor, combine the roasted tomatoes and peppers, paprika, chili flakes, and butter, and purée until smooth. Thin the mixture with as much of the remaining 3 tablespoons of olive oil as necessary. Strain the purée through a fine-mesh strainer to capture any tomato and pepper skins that may remain. Adjust the seasoning with salt, if necessary.

6. The sauce will keep in an airtight container in the refrigerator for up to 1 week or in the freezer for up to 2 months.

SUBSTITUTION TIP: *If you don't have very ripe, fresh tomatoes at your disposal, choose high-quality imported canned tomatoes such as San Marzano.*

BASIC PESTO

MAKES ABOUT 2 CUPS
Prep time: 10 minutes

There are just half a dozen ingredients in pesto, and likely ten times that many opinions on how it should be made. I'm a purist when it comes to this sauce. I don't care for additions of arugula or cilantro, or substitutions of walnuts or other nuts for pine nuts. Garlic should be present but not dominate, I prefer to leave the nuts raw, and I select only the youngest basil leaves from stalks that have not yet begun to flower. There are debates on method—blender versus mortar and pestle—that I will not weigh in on here. If time is of the essence, use a blender to make the sauce. If you want a more hands-on approach, go with the mortar and pestle. Or try both and decide for yourself, keeping in mind that heat tends to darken the sauce, so blend only as long as necessary.

1 garlic clove

Salt

2 tablespoons raw pine nuts

3 cups densely packed small, fresh basil leaves

¼ cup grated pecorino romano

1 cup extra-virgin olive oil

1. Mash the garlic with a small pinch of salt. Add the pine nuts and mash or process to a fine paste. Gradually add small handfuls of the basil to the garlic-nut paste and pound until smooth. Continue in this manner, adding basil and pounding until a smooth green paste is achieved and you have used all the basil.

2. Transfer to a small bowl and stir in the grated cheese and just enough olive oil to create a thick, herby sauce. Season with salt.

3. This sauce can be stored in an airtight container in the refrigerator for up to 2 days but is never better than when it is freshly made.

SALSA BIANCA

MAKES ABOUT 2 CUPS
Prep time: 5 minutes
Cook time: 10 minutes

This versatile white sauce complements all kinds of pizzas and calzones, particularly vegetable-based pies. Use it in the Gratin of Wild Mushroom Crèpes (page 196) as well as the Pasta al Forno (page 208). Add different grated cheeses or fresh herbs for even more varied flavors. Do not use an aluminum pot when making this sauce; it will color it an unappetizing shade of dull gray.

2½ cups whole milk

1 bay leaf

2 tablespoons unsalted butter

3 tablespoons all-purpose flour

1 cup grated Parmesan cheese

½ teaspoon salt

2 teaspoons chopped fresh thyme
(optional)

1. In a small saucepan, warm the whole milk with the bay leaf over a low flame and set aside.

2. In a stainless steel saucepan, melt the butter over a medium-low flame. When it begins to foam, add the flour all at once and whisk to avoid lumps. Cook the flour and butter mixture for 2 minutes, whisking constantly. If it begins to color, lower the flame.

3. Whisk in 1 cup of the warm milk and the bay leaf in a steady stream, making sure to thoroughly whisk the bottom of the pot to prevent scorching. Whisk in the remaining milk and lower the heat. Cook on a low simmer for 10 minutes, stirring occasionally to prevent lumps from forming. Remove from the heat, discard the bay leaf, and pass the milk mixture through a fine-mesh strainer into a bowl. Add the grated cheese, salt, and thyme, if using.

4. The sauce will thicken as it cools. Thin with a few teaspoons of milk to facilitate lining pizzas and calzones.

PREP TIP: *This recipe scales up with great success. For every extra 1 cup milk, add 1½ tablespoons flour.*

SALSA VERDE

MAKES ABOUT 1½ CUPS
Prep time: 20 minutes

Salsa verde is known far and wide as a wonderful accent to grilled or roasted meats and fish. A medley of fresh herbs, briny capers, and cured anchovies plays off the base notes that wood smoke and high heat impart to a dish. Choose the freshest herbs you can find, and prepare the salsa as close to serving time as possible; the flavors are fleeting.

1 cup finely chopped fresh flat-leaf parsley

2 tablespoons finely chopped fresh chives

2 tablespoons finely chopped chervil (optional)

1 tablespoon finely chopped fresh marjoram or oregano

1 tablespoon finely chopped fresh tarragon

1 shallot, minced

1 garlic clove, mashed to a paste

1 whole salt-packed anchovy, rinsed, soaked, filleted (see Prep Tip on page 122), and finely chopped

2 teaspoons salt-packed capers, soaked in water for 10 minutes, drained, and roughly chopped

Extra-virgin olive oil

Salt

Freshly ground black pepper

Splash of white wine vinegar

1. In a medium bowl, combine the parsley, chives, chervil (if using), marjoram, and tarragon. Add the shallot, garlic, anchovy, and capers.

2. Cover with enough olive oil to make a thick, herby sauce. Season with salt and a few grinds of pepper.

3. Just before you intend to serve the salsa, add a few drops of white wine vinegar. Taste and adjust the seasoning.

PREP TIP: *Wait until the last moment to add that splash of vinegar. This will preserve the salsa's bright green color. If the herbs begin to lose their vibrancy, the salsa will be as delicious, just slightly less eye-catching.*

WILD FENNEL SAUCE

MAKES ABOUT 1 CUP
Prep time: 15 minutes

Wild fennel has been naturalized just about everywhere in the Northern California landscape. Aromatic, anise-scented fronds dominate the hillsides, and the vibrant yellow seed heads decorate the roadsides in late summer and early fall. The stalks are wonderful for flavoring sauces, the wispy fronds are superb for marinating fish, and the flowers, filled with pollen, intensify anything they are added to. Harvest wild fennel and its flowering stalks in an area that is known to be free of chemicals or pesticides, away from busy roads if possible. Select deep green, aromatic fronds and fully blooming yellow seed heads.

½ cup finely chopped wild fennel fronds

1 tablespoon finely chopped wild fennel flowers

1 teaspoon wild fennel seed

Cayenne pepper

Salt

1 cup extra-virgin olive oil

2 garlic cloves

1. Combine the chopped fennel fronds and flowers in a bowl.

2. In a small sauté pan over low heat, lightly toast the fennel seeds. Transfer the seeds to a mortar and pestle or a spice grinder and pulverize.

3. Add the pulverized seeds to the chopped fronds and flowers. Add a small pinch of cayenne and a generous pinch of salt. Stir in the olive oil.

4. Pound the garlic cloves to a paste in the mortar and pestle and stir the paste into the fennel sauce.

5. Allow the sauce to sit at room temperature for 30 minutes for the flavors to blend. Taste and adjust with more toasted fennel seed or salt, if needed.

SUBSTITUTION TIP: *If you don't have access to wild fennel, substitute 2 tablespoons toasted fennel seeds and 1 teaspoon toasted anise seeds. Sometimes fresh fennel bulb will have the wispy fronds still attached; use those in combination with the toasted seeds.*

TAPENADE

There are as many variations on this condiment as there are varieties of cured olives. I reach for this olive paste repeatedly when I want to add a cutting, briny note to rich dishes or roasted meats and fish. It is delicious spread on North African Flatbread (page 60) or tucked into the Mediterranean-inspired Acropolis calzone (page 175).

1½ cups pitted, chopped niçoise olives

2 tablespoons salt-packed capers, rinsed, soaked, and chopped

1 shallot, minced

2 garlic cloves, mashed

1 whole salt-packed anchovy, rinsed, soaked, filleted (see Prep Tip on page 122), and minced (optional)

1 tablespoon chopped fresh flat-leaf parsley

2 teaspoons chopped fresh marjoram

1 lemon

1 orange

Extra-virgin olive oil

1. In a large bowl, combine the chopped olives, capers, shallot, mashed garlic, and anchovy, if using.

2. Add the parsley and marjoram. Using a Microplane, grate the citrus zest directly over the mixture to capture the oils in the zest.

3. Stir in just enough olive oil to make a thick, herby, slightly liquid sauce. Let stand at room temperature for 30 minutes to allow the flavors to marry.

4. The tapenade will keep for up to 1 week in an airtight container in the refrigerator.

PREP TIP: *Forgo the food processor in this preparation—instead, sharpen your knife skills and chop the ingredients by hand. You'll find that this rustic spread comes together quickly.*

AÏOLI

MAKES ABOUT 1¼ CUPS
Prep time: 15 minutes

Aïoli is the classic garlic mayonnaise that originated in Provence, France. But honestly, every culture knows how good it is. Try it with a variety of dishes, from vegetables and seafood to fried food and even the Squid Pizza with Cherry Tomatoes and Aïoli on page 130. Once you master this preparation, you'll repeatedly turn to it to add a quick kick to almost any dish.

1 extra-large egg yolk
1 teaspoon water
1 cup extra-virgin olive oil
Juice of ¼ lemon
Salt
2 garlic cloves

1. In a small bowl, whisk together the egg yolk and water, then begin drizzling in the olive oil while constantly whisking. As the mixture begins to emulsify, continue to add the oil in a thin, steady stream, whisking the entire time.

2. If the mixture becomes too thick, add a squeeze of fresh lemon juice to thin it out, then return to adding the oil and whisking. After all the oil has been incorporated, season with salt.

3. In a mortar and pestle, mash the garlic to a fine paste with a few grains of salt.

4. Add the mashed garlic to the aïoli and set aside at room temperature for 10 minutes to allow the flavors to marry. It should resemble softly whipped cream at this stage.

5. The aïoli can be stored in the refrigerator until ready to use. Add a few drops of water or lemon juice to thin the mixture if you intend to drizzle it over a pizza.

PREP TIP: *Does your aïoli look thin and separated? Don't fret, "broken" aïoli happens to the best of chefs. Here is a quick fix: Start with a clean, dry bowl and a fresh egg yolk. Slowly add the broken sauce, drop by drop, whisking constantly, until it is completely incorporated and fully emulsified.*

HARISSA

MAKES ABOUT ½ CUP
Prep time: 15 minutes

While I have never visited the spice bazaars of North Africa, when I make this delicious fiery dried pepper condiment I feel a little closer to the continent. Fragrant and heady aromas meld with the heat of raw garlic and a secondary heat from the intense dried chiles. This condiment is useful in a variety of ways, including garnishing soups, deepening marinades, slathered across roasted meats, and of course, on wood-fired flatbread.

1 teaspoon cumin seeds

1 teaspoon coriander seeds

1 teaspoon caraway seeds

½ ounce dried mild chiles, stemmed and seeded

1 tablespoon smoked paprika

½ teaspoon salt

⅛ teaspoon cayenne pepper

1 garlic clove

1 teaspoon tomato paste

⅓ cup extra-virgin olive oil

Splash of red wine vinegar

1. In a small skillet over medium-low heat, toast the cumin, coriander, and caraway seeds until fragrant, tossing frequently so they don't burn, about 3 minutes total. Transfer to a spice grinder or mortar and pestle and grind to a fine powder. Transfer to a small bowl.

2. Add the dried chiles to the spice grinder and process to a fine powder. Add to the ground seed mixture. Add the smoked paprika, salt, and cayenne.

3. Pound the garlic clove to a paste in a mortar and pestle and add to the dry spices, along with the tomato paste, olive oil, and vinegar. Gently stir with a whisk to evenly blend.

4. Transfer to a small jar and cover tightly. The condiment will keep for up to 3 days in the refrigerator.

SUBSTITUTION TIP: *This recipe calls for smoked paprika, also known as* pimentón dulce, *a delightfully rich, mahogany spice that works its way into a variety of dishes at my house. If you can't find* pimentón dulce, *use the readily available Hungarian sweet paprika in its place.*

ANCHOIADE
FIG AND ANCHOVY PASTE

MAKES ABOUT 1 CUP
Prep time: 10 minutes

This sauce is an intense blend of garlic, anchovy, and ripe figs. It may not be an everyday spread, but when the figs are plump and nearly overripe, I urge you to try this French favorite. I like the addition of fruit here; it balances the salty, oily richness of the sauce, and the whole is made more delicious with a quick turn in the wood oven atop a pizza.

4 garlic cloves, sliced

10 whole salt-packed anchovies, rinsed, soaked, and filleted (see Prep Tip on page 122)

6 fresh, ripe black Mission figs, stemmed and quartered

1 tablespoon unsalted butter, at room temperature

2 teaspoons red wine vinegar

Freshly ground black pepper

⅔ cup extra-virgin olive oil

1. In a food processor, with the motor running, drop the garlic cloves and anchovy fillets down the feed tube and chop very finely. Stop the machine once and scrape down the sides of the work bowl. Add the quartered figs and process until chopped and chunky. Add the butter, red wine vinegar, season with pepper, and process for 10 seconds longer.

2. Scrape the purée into a bowl and stir in enough olive oil to make a thick, spreadable paste. Let stand at room temperature for 30 minutes for the flavors to marry. Store in an airtight container in the refrigerator for up to 3 days.

SUBSTITUTION TIP: *Seek out black Mission figs for this recipe. Or, if you happen to have access to the green Adriatic variety, use those instead—or a mixture of both. Resist the urge to use the large and often seedy Brown Turkey figs, or any dried fruit, as the sweetness intensifies too much in the drying process.*

5 CHARCUTERIE AND MEAT PIZZAS

A TRANSFORMATION OCCURS when salt, time, and air come in contact with a humble cut of meat and a willing partner, bacteria, is allowed to thrive. A tale unfolds that could fill an entire library. Curing meats is a delicious art form, and this artisanal practice has experienced a renaissance in our recent culinary history. Seek out a retail establishment that provides a combination of house made and imported specialties of charcuterie. (Charcuterie is a French term for cold cooked or cured meats.)

The finer cuts of charcuterie are pricey for a reason: The process is time consuming and the methods are not easily reproduced. Fortunately, the following recipes require only small amounts of these specialty ingredients, yet deliver a full-flavored experience. Sample a wide array of recipes and decide what combinations you deem worthy for your pizza party night.

There are some excellent domestic producers of prosciutto in the Midwest, making hams that rival those from the storied Parma region of Italy. Spain also has a talent for producing delicious jamón, so be sure to sample offerings from there as well.

NUMBER ONE PEPPERONI PIZZA

MAKES ONE 10-INCH PIZZA
Prep time: 10 minutes
Cook time: 3 to 5 minutes

The most popular pizza the world over can now be served at your house. The final assembly of this pizza (and all the pizzas in this book) goes very quickly once the dough is proofed, so be certain all your ingredients are cooked and/or chopped, the dough is ready, and your guests are hungry. As you assemble the pizza, be careful not to spill toppings or sauce over the edges. A sloppy peel inhibits sliding the pizza cleanly into the oven.

> 1 portion Basic Go-To Easy Pizza Dough (page 49)
>
> 2 tablespoons Essential Garlic Oil (page 69), plus more for finishing
>
> ½ cup Oven-Roasted Red Sauce (page 71)
>
> ½ cup shredded part-skim mozzarella
>
> Salt
>
> 2 ounces highest-quality pepperoni, thinly sliced
>
> Parmesan cheese

1. Following the directions for a fully prepped oven, make sure your fire is at the desired cooking temperature with a roiling flame and a brushed and cleaned oven floor. You are now ready to make a pizza.

2. Stretch out the dough as shown in "How to Shape a Pizza" (page 51). Lightly dust your pizza peel with flour. Place your stretched dough directly on the peel and proceed to build the pizza.

3. Brush the stretched dough with the garlic oil and spread the oven-roasted tomato sauce evenly over the dough, leaving a ½-inch border all the way around the outside. Top the pie with the shredded mozzarella. Season the entire pie with a pinch of salt.

4. Scatter the pepperoni slices. Be generous with the pepperoni so everyone gets his or her fill in each bite.

5. Slide the pizza into the oven and bake for 3 to 5 minutes, rotating once or twice to ensure even cooking. Remove the pizza to a cutting board. Slice into 6 or 8 wedges. Grate Parmesan over the entire pie. Brush the crust edges with a quick pass of garlic oil to finish.

PIZZA WITH PROSCIUTTO CRUDO, RICOTTA, AND AGED BALSAMICO

MAKES ONE 10-INCH PIZZA
Prep time: 10 minutes
Cook time: 3 to 5 minutes

Crudo in Italian translates as "raw," which describes the state of the ham when it was butchered and hung to cure. The magic of Parma prosciutto is in the drying process, whereby an entire hog leg is transformed, with the aid of bacteria, into something extraordinary. There's no cooking involved—just months to years of dry curing.

½ cup fresh ricotta

Salt

1 tablespoon extra-virgin olive oil

1 portion Elevated Pizza Dough (page 52)

3 tablespoons Essential Garlic Oil (page 69), plus more for finishing

¼ cup Oven-Roasted Red Sauce (page 71)

½ cup arugula

4 slices prosciutto crudo

Freshly ground black pepper

1 teaspoon aged balsamic vinegar

1. In a small bowl, whisk the ricotta to smooth the curds. Season with a pinch of salt and stir in the olive oil.

2. Following the directions for a fully prepped oven, make sure your fire is at the desired cooking temperature with a roiling flame and a brushed and cleaned oven floor. You are now ready to make a pizza.

3. Stretch out the dough as shown in "How to Shape a Pizza" (page 51). Lightly dust your pizza peel with flour. Place your stretched dough directly on the peel and proceed to build the pizza.

4. Brush the stretched dough with the garlic oil and spread the whisked ricotta evenly over the dough, leaving a ½-inch border all the way around the outside. Top the ricotta with the red sauce, followed by the arugula. Season the entire pie with a pinch of salt.

5. Slide the pizza into the oven and bake for 3 to 5 minutes, rotating once or twice to ensure even cooking. Remove the pizza to a cutting board.

6. Drape the prosciutto slices over the cooked pizza and add a few grinds of black pepper. Drizzle the entire pie with the aged *balsamico*. Slice into 6 or 8 wedges. Brush the crust edges with a quick pass of garlic oil to finish.

PIZZA WITH PROSCIUTTO COTTO AND GORGONZOLA

MAKES ONE 10-INCH PIZZA

Prep time: 10 minutes
Cook time: 3 to 5 minutes

Cotto in Italian translates as "cooked," which means the ham was cooked rather than cured and aged in the style of prosciutto *crudo*. This preparation yields a finished product that lacks the intense concentrated flavor of its *crudo* brother and reveals more of the sweet, fatty American-style ham. It works well when combined with cheese, then cooked in a fiery oven.

1 portion Elevated Pizza Dough (page 52)

3 tablespoons Essential Garlic Oil (page 69), plus more for finishing

½ cup Salsa Bianca (page 75)

3 ounces prosciutto cotto, thinly sliced

¼ cup crumbled Gorgonzola

Salt

2 tablespoons chopped fresh flat-leaf parsley

½ teaspoon freshly squeezed lemon juice

½ teaspoon extra-virgin olive oil

Freshly ground black pepper

1. Following the directions for a fully prepped oven, make sure your fire is at the desired cooking temperature with a roiling flame and a brushed and cleaned oven floor. You are now ready to make a pizza.

2. Stretch out the dough as shown in "How to Shape a Pizza" (page 51). Lightly dust your pizza peel with flour. Place your stretched dough directly on the peel and proceed to build the pizza.

3. Brush the stretched dough with the garlic oil and spread the salsa bianca evenly over the dough, leaving a ½-inch border all the way around the outside. Top the pie with the prosciutto slices and crumble on the Gorgonzola. Season the entire pie with a pinch of salt.

4. Slide the pizza into the oven and bake for 3 to 5 minutes, rotating once or twice to ensure even cooking. Remove the pizza to a cutting board.

5. Toss the parsley leaves with a squeeze of lemon juice and a few drops of olive oil, add a few grinds of black pepper, and scatter over the pie. Slice into 6 or 8 wedges. Brush the crust edges with a quick pass of garlic oil to finish.

PANCETTA PIZZA WITH SWISS CHARD AND ONIONS

MAKES ONE 10-INCH PIZZA
Prep time: 20 minutes
Cook time: 20 to 25 minutes

Wilted greens, soft onions, and a punctuation of peppery, cured pancetta would make a delicious side dish to almost any entrée, so why not enjoy the flavors together on a pizza pie? I like to use a cheese that melts well but also carries with it a bit more depth of flavor than say, mozzarella; aged Gruyère is an ideal partner.

1 yellow onion, diced

1 bunch Swiss chard, leaves stripped from stems, stems reserved (optional)

2 tablespoons extra-virgin olive oil, divided

Salt

1 portion Basic Go-To Easy Pizza Dough (page 49)

3 tablespoons Essential Garlic Oil (page 69), plus more for finishing

½ cup Simple Tomato Sauce (page 70)

½ cup shredded Gruyère cheese

4 thin slices pancetta

Freshly ground black pepper

1. Following the directions for a fully prepped oven, make sure your fire is at the desired cooking temperature with a roiling flame and a brushed and cleaned oven floor. You are now ready to make a pizza.

2. Combine the yellow onion dice with the chard stems, if using, in a cast iron skillet, and season with 1 tablespoon of olive oil and a pinch of salt. Sauté the vegetables slowly, in the window of the oven, until tender, about 8 minutes. Set aside until ready to use.

3. Repeat with the chard leaves in the same manner, seasoning with the remaining 1 tablespoon of olive oil and a pinch of salt and sautéing slowly until wilted. Stir often to prevent burning, and add a splash of water if the pan dries out. Combine the onion-stem mixture and the cooked chard.

4. Stretch out the dough as shown in "How to Shape a Pizza" (page 51). Lightly dust your pizza peel with flour. Place your stretched dough directly on the peel and proceed to build the pizza.

5. Brush the stretched dough with the garlic oil and spread the tomato sauce evenly over the dough, leaving a ½-inch border all the way around the outside. Arrange the Gruyère over the dough, followed by the greens mixture. Take care not to overload the pizza. Season the pie with a pinch of salt. Drape the pancetta slices over the pie.

6. Slide the pizza into the oven and bake for 3 to 5 minutes, rotating once or twice to ensure even cooking.

7. Remove the pizza to a cutting board and add a few grinds of black pepper. Slice into 6 or 8 wedges. Brush the crust edges with a quick pass of garlic oil to finish.

A CLOSER LOOK: *Pancetta is simply unsmoked bacon. Cured with salt, black pepper, and warm spices, it is the belly of the pork rolled into a log, tied, and dried for a short period of time. There really is no substitute for the sweet and savory flavor pancetta brings to a dish.*

PIZZA WITH FENNEL SAUSAGE, PEPPERS, AND CALABRIAN CHILES

MAKES ONE 10-INCH PIZZA

Prep time: 20 minutes
Cook time: about 10 minutes

Sausage and peppers always reminds me of the oversized sandwiches you can get "down the shore" on the boardwalks of New Jersey. Heaped with onions and dressed with a spicy pickled condiment made from puréed Calabrian hot peppers, they would make you forget the hours of traffic that lay ahead just to get back home.

¾ cup thinly sliced sweet bell peppers

1 yellow onion, thinly sliced

Extra-virgin olive oil

Salt

4 ounces fennel sausage, casing removed, crumbled

1 portion Basic Go-To Easy Pizza Dough (page 49)

2 tablespoons Essential Garlic Oil (page 69), plus more for finishing

¼ cup Simple Tomato Sauce (page 70)

½ cup shredded part-skim mozzarella

1 tablespoon Calabrian chile purée (see A Closer Look)

2 tablespoons flat-leaf Italian parsley

1. Combine the peppers and onion in a small bowl, moisten with enough olive oil to thoroughly coat the vegetables, and season with salt. Set aside to soften slightly for 10 minutes.

2. Following the directions for a fully prepped oven, make sure your fire is at the desired cooking temperature with a roiling flame and a brushed and cleaned oven floor.

3. Place the crumbled fennel sausage in a cast iron skillet and brown in the oven, about 5 minutes. Remove from the pan and drain the fat.

4. Stretch out the dough as shown in "How to Shape a Pizza" (page 51). Lightly dust your pizza peel with flour. Place your stretched dough directly on the peel and proceed to build the pizza.

5. Brush the stretched dough with the garlic oil and spread the tomato sauce evenly over the dough, leaving a ½-inch border all the way around the outside. Top the pie with the mozzarella cheese. Season the entire pie with a pinch of salt. →

6. Lift the peppers and onions from the bowl and allow any excess liquid to drain off. Spread evenly over the pizza. Arrange the crumbled sausage over the pie.

7. Slide the pizza into the oven and bake for 3 to 5 minutes, rotating once or twice to ensure even cooking. Remove the pizza to a cutting board. Slice into 6 or 8 wedges.

8. In a thin drizzle, garnish the cooked pizza with the Calabrian chile purée. Brush the crust edges with a quick pass of garlic oil to finish. Garnish with the parsley leaves.

A CLOSER LOOK: *Jarred Calabrian chile purée is available online and in specialty markets. Choose the hot kind, and pick a brand that has minimal ingredients—I like the Crushed Hot Chili Peppers from Tutto Calabria. You will spread this condiment on every-thing, guaranteed.*

QUATTRO STAGIONI
FOUR SEASONS PIZZA

MAKES ONE 6-BY-12-INCH PIZZA
Prep time: 30 minutes
Cook time: about 10 minutes

There is a little something for everyone on this pizza: earthy mushrooms, smoky ham, herby pesto, and the salinity of cured anchovies. Now that you have mastered tossing a perfectly round pizza, challenge yourself to make a long rectangle with this dough. Divide the elongated pizza into four distinct sections by garnishing each quadrant with a single topping, and eat your way through the seasons one bite at a time!

½ cup wild mushrooms such as black trumpets or chanterelles

Extra-virgin olive oil

Salt

1 portion Basic Go-To Easy Pizza Dough (page 49)

1 tablespoon Essential Garlic Oil (page 69), plus more for finishing

¾ cup Simple Tomato Sauce (page 70)

¼ cup Basic Pesto (page 74)

¾ cup shredded part-skim mozzarella

2 fresh basil leaves

2 whole salt-packed anchovy fillets, rinsed, soaked, filleted (see Prep Tip on page 122), and halved lengthwise (8 pieces total)

2 ounces smoked ham, thinly sliced

1 ounce crumbled Gorgonzola

Parmesan cheese

Freshly ground black pepper →

1. Toss the mushrooms with a little olive oil and salt and roast them in a cazuela in the oven until they are wilted and slightly caramelized, about 7 minutes. Set aside to cool.

2. Following the directions for a fully prepped oven, make sure your fire is at the desired cooking temperature with a roiling flame and a brushed and cleaned oven floor. You are now ready to make a pizza.

3. Stretch out the dough as shown in "How to Shape a Pizza" (page 51). Lightly dust your pizza peel with flour. Place your stretched dough directly on the peel and proceed to build the pizza.

4. Brush the stretched dough with the garlic oil and spread the tomato sauce evenly over three-quarters of the dough, leaving a ½-inch border. Spread the pesto over the last quarter of the dough. Arrange the shredded mozzarella over the entire pie. Garnish the pesto portion with the basil leaves.

Garnish another quarter with the anchovy fillets, and another with the cooked wild mushrooms. For the last quarter, lay down the ham slices and dot with the Gorgonzola. You should have four distinct sections.

5. Slide the pizza into the oven and bake for 3 to 5 minutes, rotating once or twice to ensure even cooking. Remove the pizza to a cutting board, grate Parmesan over the entire pie, and add a few grinds of black pepper. Slice into four quarters and those quarters into bite-size pieces for all to enjoy. Brush the crust edges with a quick pass of garlic oil to finish.

PREP TIP: *Try using a rolling pin to shape the dough into a rough rectangle, making sure it will fit on your peel to deliver it to the oven. Or, build the Four Seasons directly onto the bottom of a well-floured half sheet and slide it into the oven quickly and easily.*

SALAMI PIZZA WITH PARSLEY-PARMESAN SALAD

MAKES ONE 10-INCH PIZZA
Prep time: 10 minutes
Cook time: 3 to 5 minutes

This pizza is a hands-down winner. Whether it is the cheesy-topped dough laden with burnt-edge salami or the refreshing herb salad that lands upon it, you will debate the divine simplicity. Since there is a minimal number of ingredients on this pie, purchase the best salami you can find. Supplement it by using fresh Italian parsley and authentic Parmigiano-Reggiano.

1 portion Basic Go-To Easy Pizza Dough (page 49)

3 tablespoons Essential Garlic Oil (page 69), plus more for finishing

½ cup Oven-Roasted Red Sauce (page 71)

½ cup shredded part-skim mozzarella

10 thin slices imported dry salami, preferably Tuscan-style

½ cup fresh flat-leaf parsley leaves

¼ cup shredded Parmesan cheese

Salt

Extra-virgin olive oil

1. Following the directions for a fully prepped oven, make sure your fire is at the desired cooking temperature with a roiling flame and a brushed and cleaned oven floor. You are now ready to make a pizza.

2. Stretch out the dough as shown in "How to Shape a Pizza" (page 51). Lightly dust your pizza peel with flour. Place your stretched dough directly on the peel and proceed to build the pizza.

3. Brush the stretched dough with the garlic oil and spread the red sauce over the dough, leaving a ½-inch border. Top with the shredded mozzarella and the thinly sliced salami, covering the entire surface of the pie by overlapping the salami rounds.

4. Slide the pizza into the oven and bake for 3 to 5 minutes, rotating once or twice to ensure even cooking. Remove the pizza to a cutting board and cut into 6 to 8 wedges. Brush the crust edges with a quick pass of garlic oil to finish.

5. In a small bowl, toss the parsley and Parmesan together, then dress with a pinch of salt and a few drops of olive oil. Mound the parsley salad in the center of the pizza and encourage guests to get a bit of green with every slice they enjoy.

FENNEL SAUSAGE AND WILTED GREENS PIZZA WITH FRESH MOZZARELLA

MAKES ONE 10-INCH PIZZA
Prep time: 20 minutes
Cook time: 25 minutes

If you can find a good source for fennel sausage—or even venture to make your own—use it here as well as in the Pizza with Fennel Sausage, Peppers, and Calabrian Chiles (page 91). The slight nuttiness of the whole-wheat dough is a delicious complement to the richness of the fennel sausage and the healthful greens. The fresh mozzarella can be heavy on soft crust pizzas, so be sure to slice it very thinly.

1 yellow onion, diced

1 bunch Swiss chard, leaves stripped from stems, stems reserved (optional)

2 tablespoons extra-virgin olive oil, divided

Salt

4 ounces fennel sausage, casing removed, crumbled

1 portion Whole-Wheat Pizza Dough (page 56)

2 tablespoons Essential Garlic Oil (page 69), plus more for finishing

¼ cup Simple Tomato Sauce (page 70)

4 ounces buffalo mozzarella, thinly sliced

1. Following the directions for a fully prepped oven, make sure your fire is at the desired cooking temperature with a roiling flame and a brushed and cleaned oven floor. You are now ready to make a pizza.

2. Combine the yellow onion dice with the chard stems, if using, in a cast iron skillet, and season with 1 tablespoon of olive oil and a pinch of salt. Sauté the vegetables slowly, in the window of the oven, until tender, about 8 minutes. Set aside until ready to use.

3. Repeat with the chard leaves in the same manner, seasoning and sautéing slowly until wilted. Stir often to prevent burning and add a splash of water if the pan dries out. Combine the onion-stem mixture and the cooked chard.

4. Place the crumbled fennel sausage in a cast iron skillet and brown in the oven, about 5 minutes. Remove from the pan and drain the fat.

5. Stretch out the dough as shown in "How to Shape a Pizza" (page 51). Lightly dust your pizza peel with flour. Place your stretched dough directly on the peel and proceed to build the pizza.

6. Brush the stretched dough with the garlic oil and spread the tomato sauce evenly over the dough, leaving a ½-inch border all the way around the outside. Top the pie with the vegetable mixture and the sliced mozzarella cheese. Season the entire pie with a pinch of salt. Arrange the crumbled sausage over the greens and cheese.

7. Slide the pizza into the oven and bake for 3 to 5 minutes, rotating once or twice to ensure even cooking. Remove the pizza to a cutting board. Slice into 6 or 8 wedges. Brush the crust edges with a quick pass of garlic oil to finish.

WHOLE-WHEAT PIZZA WITH PANCETTA, POTATO, AND ASPARAGUS

MAKES TWO 6-INCH PIZZAS

Prep time: 30 minutes

Cook time: about 10 minutes per pizza

These mini pies are great for a kids' snack or even as a starter for a casual cocktail hour. If you went to the trouble of firing up the wood oven and plan on creating a dinner party that is beyond pizza, consider starting with these quick little pizzas for a few savory hors d'oeuvres.

8 ounces Yellow Finn potatoes, sliced ⅛ inch thick

Salt

Extra-virgin olive oil

2 thick asparagus spears

1 portion Whole-Wheat Pizza Dough (page 56), divided into two equal balls

2 tablespoons Essential Garlic Oil (page 69), plus more for finishing

½ cup Salsa Bianca (page 75)

½ cup shredded Fontina cheese

6 ounces pancetta, thinly sliced

Parmesan cheese

Freshly ground black pepper

1. Following the directions for a fully prepped oven, make sure your fire is at the desired cooking temperature with a roiling flame and a brushed and cleaned oven floor.

2. In a bowl, toss the potato slices with a generous pinch of salt and moisten with a splash each of olive oil and water. Arrange the potatoes in a single layer on an unlined half sheet pan and roast in a very hot oven until they begin to take on color and soften, 4 to 7 minutes. Allow the potatoes to cool completely, taste, and adjust the seasoning with more salt if needed. Set aside until you're ready to build the pizza.

3. Prepare the asparagus by snapping off the woody stems and discarding. Using a mandoline, carefully slice the raw asparagus lengthwise, creating paper-thin ribbons. Toss the asparagus ribbons in a small bowl with a splash of oil and a pinch of salt.

4. Stretch out one piece of dough as shown in "How to Shape a Pizza" (page 51). Lightly dust your pizza peel with flour. Place your stretched dough directly on the peel and proceed to build the pizza.

5. Brush the stretched dough with the garlic oil and spread half of the salsa bianca over the pizza. Distribute half of the shredded Fontina evenly over the dough, leaving a ½-inch border all the way around the outside. Add half of the cooked potato slices and half of the asparagus to the pie. Season with a pinch of salt. Top with half of the pancetta.

6. Slide the pizza into the oven and bake for 3 to 5 minutes, rotating once or twice to ensure even cooking. Remove the pizza to a cutting board, grate Parmesan cheese over the entire pie, and add a few grinds of black pepper. Slice into 4 wedges. Brush the crust edges with a quick pass of garlic oil to finish.

7. Repeat with the second pizza.

BREAKFAST PIE
APPLEWOOD SMOKED BACON AND SUNNY-SIDE UP EGGS WITH PARMESAN

MAKES ONE 10-INCH PIZZA
Prep time: 10 minutes
Cook time: 5 to 7 minutes

The idea of breakfast in Italy is a cappuccino and a brioche—coffee and a croissant-like pastry, filled with sweet jam. The idea of breakfast in my house is bacon and eggs. Why not on a pizza, paired with a large press pot of coffee?

1 portion Whole-Wheat Pizza Dough (page 56)

1 tablespoon Essential Garlic Oil (page 69), plus more for finishing

½ cup Salsa Bianca (page 75)

¼ cup shredded part-skim mozzarella

½ cup thinly sliced red onion

4 ounces uncooked thinly sliced applewood smoked bacon or precooked thicker bacon

2 eggs

Salt

Parmesan cheese

Freshly ground black pepper

1. Following the directions for a fully prepped oven, make sure your fire is at the desired cooking temperature with a roiling flame and a brushed and cleaned oven floor. You are now ready to make a pizza.

2. Stretch out the dough as shown in "How to Shape a Pizza" (page 51). Lightly dust your pizza peel with flour. Place your stretched dough directly on the peel and proceed to build the pizza.

3. Brush the stretched dough with the garlic oil and spread the salsa bianca over the dough, leaving a ½-inch border. Top with the shredded mozzarella and the thinly sliced onion, followed by the uncooked bacon (if using).

4. Slide the pizza into the oven and bake for 2 minutes to set the bottom of the pie. Remove from the oven and crack the eggs carefully onto the pizza. Season the eggs with salt. Return to the oven and cook for 3 to 5 minutes longer, rotating once or twice to ensure even cooking. Remove the pizza to a cutting board when the bacon has cooked through and the egg whites are set but the yolks remain soft.

5. Grate Parmesan cheese over the entire pie and add a few grinds of black pepper. Garnish with the precooked bacon (if using). Brush the crust edges with a quick pass of the garlic oil to finish. Enjoy as a proper breakfast, with a knife and fork.

PREP TIP: *If you can, have your butcher slice the bacon. Very thin is what you want, so it cooks in the time it takes the pizza to finish in the oven. If you are going with store-bought bacon, precook it and garnish the pie when it comes out of the oven.*

PIZZA WITH CHORIZO Y PAPAS, FRESH CILANTRO, AND LIME

MAKES ONE 10-INCH PIZZA
Prep time: 40 minutes
Cook time: 30 minutes

These are flavors lifted right out of the taquerias where I live. The deep spices of Mexican-style chorizo sausage cooked together with starchy potatoes and brightened by lots of cilantro and a squeeze of lime may make you rethink a traditional pizza. Enjoy this pie with plenty of ice-cold Mexican beer.

1 russet potato, peeled and cut into ½-inch dice

4 ounces Mexican-style chorizo, crumbled

1 portion Basic Go-To Easy Pizza Dough (page 49) or Spelt Pizza Dough (page 54)

2 ounces Cotija cheese, crumbled

2 tablespoons crème fraîche

¼ cup chopped fresh cilantro leaves and stems

1 lime

1. Cook the potato in boiling salted water until tender, about 10 minutes. Drain well and reserve.

2. Preheat a cast iron skillet for 5 minutes in the wood oven, add the chorizo, and cook in a medium-hot environment for 3 minutes to render some of the fat. Add the cooked potato to the skillet, stir to combine, and return to the oven. Continue to cook until the chorizo is cooked through and the potatoes receive some color, about 3 minutes more. Remove and set aside to cool completely.

3. Following the directions for a fully prepped oven, make sure your fire is at the desired cooking temperature with a roiling flame and a brushed and cleaned oven floor. You are now ready to make a pizza.

4. Stretch out the dough as shown in "How to Shape a Pizza" (page 51). Lightly dust your pizza peel with flour. Place your stretched dough directly on the peel and proceed to build the pizza.

5. Spread the chorizo and potato mixture over the stretched pizza crust in a thin, even layer, leaving a ½-inch border around the pizza. Top with the crumbled Cotija cheese.

6. Slide the pizza into the oven and bake for 3 to 5 minutes, rotating once or twice to ensure even cooking. Remove the pizza to a cutting board, drizzle the crème fraîche over the pie, garnish with the fresh cilantro, and squeeze a bit of lime juice over it all. Slice into 6 or 8 wedges.

A CLOSER LOOK: *The search for authentic chorizo is another opportunity to connect with the merchants in your town. It may be that your local butcher or Whole Foods Market carries chorizo, but also explore some of the Latin American markets that surely exist near you. Almost always, there is a butcher counter in the back that services the community with staples that aren't available in chain stores.*

PIZZA WITH LAMB SAUSAGE, CARAMELIZED ONIONS, AND MARJORAM

MAKES ONE 10-INCH PIZZA
Prep time: 35 minutes
Cook time: 30 minutes

Artisan butcher shops have burst onto the scene in recent years—an example of when a formerly down-trodden part of town has turned the corner and become a trendy locale. Say what you will about gentrification and redevelopment, but with it come better shopping and dining options. Seek out your neighborhood butcher and ask for an uncomplicated lamb sausage, something made with good pork back fat, garlic, and herbs like sage or rosemary. Establish a relation-ship with the counterperson and support local independent busi-nesses. You can always find a more generic product at your local Whole Foods Market, as well.

2 yellow onions, thinly sliced
2 tablespoons extra-virgin olive oil
Salt
4 ounces lamb sausage
1 portion Elevated Pizza Dough (page 52)
1 tablespoon Essential Garlic Oil (page 69), plus more for finishing
½ cup Charred Sweet Pepper and Tomato Sauce (page 72)
½ cup shredded part-skim mozzarella
Freshly ground black pepper
2 tablespoons roughly chopped fresh marjoram

1. Following the directions for a fully prepped oven, make sure your fire is at the desired cooking temperature, with a roiling flame and a brushed and cleaned oven floor.

2. Toss the onion slices with the olive oil and salt in a cazuela and roast slowly in the mouth of the oven, tossing frequently. Prevent the onions from burning by adding a splash of water if needed. The onions will lose considerable volume, begin to color slightly, and become much sweeter. When the onions have deeply colored and lost most of their volume, after 20 minutes or so, remove the pan. Allow to cool.

3. Meanwhile, remove the sausage from its casing and crumble into a cast iron skillet. Roast in the oven until the fat begins to render and the meat colors slightly, 3 to 4 minutes. Remove from the skillet, drain the fat, and set aside.

4. Stretch out the dough as shown in "How to Shape a Pizza" (page 51). Lightly dust your pizza peel with flour. Place your stretched dough directly on the peel and proceed to build the pizza.

5. Brush the stretched dough with the garlic oil and spread the pepper and tomato sauce evenly over the dough, leaving a ½-inch border all the way around the outside. Arrange the shredded cheese on top, distributing evenly.

6. Spread the caramelized onions over the cheese, crumble over the partially cooked lamb sausage, then season the entire pie with a pinch of salt.

7. Slide the pizza into the oven and bake for 3 to 5 minutes, rotating once or twice to ensure even cooking. Remove the pizza to a cutting board and add a few grinds of black pepper. Garnish with the chopped marjoram. Slice into 6 or 8 wedges. Brush the crust edges with a quick pass of the garlic oil to finish.

FLAMMEKEUCHE
ALSATIAN-STYLE TART OF STEWED ONIONS, BACON LARDONS, AND BLACK PEPPER

MAKES ONE 12-BY-18-INCH TART
Prep time: 40 minutes
Cook time: 25 minutes

The name of this traditional Alsatian-style pizza translates loosely as "tart on fire," which presumably suggests cooking it in a wood-fired oven. Variations abound, but if you go with the basics—onions, bacon lardons, fromage blanc, and black pepper—you will be honoring the origins of the dish. Try baking it in a rectangular sheet tray for further authenticity.

4 medium yellow onions, thinly sliced

Extra-virgin olive oil

1 tablespoon salt

¼ cup Alsatian white wine or German-style pilsner beer (optional)

2 portions Basic Go-To Easy Pizza Dough (page 49)

8 ounces Gruyère cheese, shredded

1 pound smoked bacon, cut into 1-inch lardons, rendered until slightly crispy, and drained on a paper towel

¼ cup crème fraîche

1 cup fromage blanc cheese

Freshly ground black pepper

1. Toss the onions with enough olive oil to moisten and season with the salt. Transfer to a cazuela large enough to hold the onions in a single layer and slowly roast in the window of the wood oven for about 15 minutes, stirring often. The idea is to soften the onions but avoid coloring them too much. Add wine, beer, or water if the edges begin to brown too quickly, or if the cazuela dries out. When sufficiently softened, remove from the oven and allow to cool.

2. Brush a half sheet pan with a small amount of olive oil and stretch the dough as outlined in the recipe for Rosemary Focaccia (page 62). Gradually press the dough into the corners of the pan, eventually filling in the entire rectangle. Allow the dough to rest a few minutes if you are having trouble stretching it and filling in the form.

3. Top the dough with the onions, followed by the Gruyère. Arrange the bacon lardons and press them lightly into the onion mixture. Drizzle the tart with the crème fraîche and finally top with small spoonfuls of the fromage blanc.

4. In a medium-hot oven, bake the tart, rotating often until the dough sets, the onions begin to color, and the bacon crisps. Check to see that the crust is browning nicely by lifting the dough with a spatula. If the tart seems to be cooking too quickly, move the pan to the window where it can cook more slowly and steadily. The total cooking time should be under 10 minutes.

5. If you desire a firm, crisp crust, carefully slide the dough from the pan and finish directly on the hearth floor until crisped and browned.

6. Remove from the oven, transfer to a cutting board, and cut into equal squares. Finish with a generous grinding of black pepper.

WHAT TO DRINK: *A crisp Alsatian white wine, served cold, or German-style pilsner beer, would complement this dish greatly.*

FENNEL PIZZA WITH BRESAOLA AND LEMON

MAKES ONE 10-INCH PIZZA
Prep time: 10 minutes
Cook time: 3 to 5 minutes

I've taken risks to eat bresaola, an air-dried, lightly spiced beef, that butchers refer to as "eye of round." It's an often forgettable cut of meat that, in capable hands, transforms into something ethereal. It may seem like an exaggeration, but try well-made bresaola, sliced paper thin, dressed in lemony vinaigrette with its jerky-like, gamy sweetness, and you too will be a disciple. This pizza turns out to be more of a vehicle for enjoying this decadent ingredient than a proper pie; it's delicious nonetheless.

1 portion Elevated Pizza Dough (page 52)

½ cup Wild Fennel Sauce (page 77)

1 cup very thinly sliced fennel
    bulb, divided

Salt

10 thin slices bresaola

Juice of ½ lemon

Parmesan cheese

Freshly ground black pepper

1. Following the directions for a fully prepped oven, make sure your fire is at the desired cooking temperature with a roiling flame and a brushed and cleaned oven floor. You are now ready to make a pizza.

2. Stretch out the dough as shown in "How to Shape a Pizza" (page 51). Lightly dust your pizza peel with flour. Place your stretched dough directly on the peel and proceed to build the pizza.

3. Spread the fennel sauce generously over the dough, leaving a ½-inch border. In a small bowl, toss half of the sliced fennel with a generous pinch of salt and spread evenly over the dough.

4. Slide the pizza into the oven and bake for 3 to 5 minutes, rotating once or twice to ensure even cooking. Remove the pizza to a cutting board and garnish with the bresaola slices. Slice into 6 or 8 wedges.

5. Dress the remaining fennel slices with the lemon juice and salt, and heap on the pizza. Grate Parmesan over the entire pie and add a few grinds of black pepper.

MERGUEZ FLATBREAD WITH ZUCCHINI, SMOKY EGGPLANT, AND CILANTRO

MAKES ONE 10-INCH FLATBREAD

Prep time: 1 hour
Cook time: 3 to 5 minutes

Merguez is a wonderful North African ground lamb sausage that is generously spiced with paprika. This pizza is well balanced between the heat of the harissa that sauces it and the cooling cilantro that ties together the veggies and lamb. This flatbread uses half of the recipe for Eggplant Roasted in the Coals (page 198) as a topping. Make the whole thing and use the rest for an appetizer the following day.

1 portion North African Flatbread dough (page 60), omitting the za'atar

¼ cup Harissa (page 80)

½ cup very thinly sliced zucchini

½ recipe Eggplant Roasted in the Coals (page 198)

4 ounces merguez sausage, casing removed, crumbled

Salt

¼ cup chopped fresh cilantro

2 tablespoons crème fraîche

1. Following the directions for a fully prepped oven, make sure your fire is at the desired cooking temperature with a roiling flame and a brushed and cleaned oven floor. You are now ready to make a flatbread pizza.

2. Follow the instructions as outlined in the North African Flatbread recipe for shaping. Stretch out the dough as shown in "How to Shape a Pizza" (page 51). Lightly dust your pizza peel with flour. Place your stretched dough directly on the peel and proceed to build the pizza.

3. Brush the stretched dough with the harissa and spread out the zucchini on the pizza, leaving a ½-inch border all the way around the outside. Spread the eggplant purée in between the zucchini on the exposed dough. Dot the crumbled merguez in the remaining exposed spaces of the flatbread. Season the entire pie with a pinch of salt.

4. Slide the pizza into the oven and bake for 3 to 5 minutes, rotating once or twice to ensure even cooking. Remove the pizza to a cutting board, scatter the cilantro over the pie, and drizzle with the crème fraîche. Slice into 6 or 8 wedges.

6 POULTRY AND SEAFOOD PIZZAS

"ONE IF BY LAND, TWO IF BY SEA" was the signal Paul Revere was looking for on his historic midnight ride—the signal to be sent based on the movements of the invading British army. It may be worth borrowing the call to arms to alert your guests that savory poultry and seafood pizzas are now being served. You may not have thought about seafood on pizzas, beyond anchovies. But seafood, particularly shellfish, lends itself to the high, dry heat of the wood-fired oven, thanks in part to its quick cooking time and an affinity for wood smoke and the charred flavor that fire endows.

As with selecting quality produce and meat, use a discerning eye when selecting poultry and seafood. Find a reliable source for organic chicken, one that uses unadulterated feed, is free of growth hormones, and ideally allows for a free-range life cycle. Our oceans are being increasingly overfished and polluted, which is all the more reason to make conscious consumer decisions when you purchase seafood. I prefer fresh to frozen and, whenever possible, fish that is harvested sustainably. Here is an opportunity to create a relationship with your local fishmongers. Ask that they support sustainable fishing, discuss seasonal runs, and even talk about how best to prepare the catch of the day.

PIZZA WITH CHICKEN SAUSAGE, RED ONIONS, AND CHARRED SWEET PEPPER AND TOMATO SAUCE

MAKES ONE 10-INCH PIZZA

Prep time: 30 minutes
Cook time: 3 to 5 minutes

When I considered writing a pizza cookbook, I had more than a few opinions about what does and does not belong on a pizza. Chicken as a topping was something that seemed dull and should be left to those "take and bake" chains that advertise during televised sports. However, it turns out that chicken can be delicious as a pizza topping when used sparingly and cooked quickly to avoid becoming dry and chewy. Chicken sausage ensures that the naturally lean meat is partnered with juicy fat and cooks up moist.

1 portion Basic Go-To Easy Pizza Dough (page 49)

2 tablespoons Essential Garlic Oil (page 69), plus more for finishing

½ cup Charred Sweet Pepper and Tomato Sauce (page 72)

½ cup shredded part-skim mozzarella

1 red onion, thinly sliced on a mandoline

Salt

1 teaspoon finely chopped fresh rosemary

Extra-virgin olive oil

4 ounces chicken sausage, casing removed, crumbled

Parmesan cheese

Freshly ground black pepper

1. Following the directions for a fully prepped oven, make sure your fire is at the desired cooking temperature with a roiling flame and a brushed and cleaned oven floor. You are now ready to make a pizza.

2. Stretch out the dough as shown in "How to Shape a Pizza" (page 51). Lightly dust your pizza peel with flour. Place your stretched dough directly on the peel and proceed to build the pizza. →

3. Brush the stretched dough with the garlic oil and spread the pepper and tomato sauce evenly, leaving a ½-inch border all the way around the outside. Distribute the shredded mozzarella cheese evenly over the pizza.

4. In a small bowl, toss the sliced red onion with a pinch of salt, the chopped rosemary, and a splash of olive oil.

5. Arrange the onion-herb mixture over the cheese. Fill in the spaces with the crumbled chicken sausage. Sprinkle the entire pie with a pinch of salt.

6. Slide the pizza into the oven and bake for 3 to 5 minutes, rotating once or twice to ensure even cooking. Remove the pizza to a cutting board, grate Parmesan cheese over the entire pie, and add a few grinds of black pepper. Slice into 6 or 8 wedges. Brush the crust edges with a quick pass of the garlic oil to finish.

A CLOSER LOOK: *Chicken sausage is now available at most well-appointed supermarkets. Select a simple preparation consisting of herbs and spices and a mixture of leg, thigh, and breast meat.*

PIZZA WITH SAN MARZANO TOMATOES AND BRAISED CHICKEN LEGS

MAKES ONE 10-INCH PIZZA

Prep time: 20 minutes for the braise, 15 minutes for the pizza

Cook time: 1 hour 10 minutes for the braise, 3 to 5 minutes for the pizza

This is a winter pizza that combines imported canned tomatoes and tender braised dark-meat chicken. If you happen to have canned some tomatoes during the summer's peak, this is a great use for them. Rather than saucing the pizza, crush the whole tomatoes by hand, then scatter them over the pizza for big, juicy bites in every slice. Start two days before you plan to make this pizza: Season the chicken legs on day one, braise them on day two, and build your pizza on day three.

FOR THE BRAISE

2 organic bone-in, skin-on whole chicken legs

Salt

Freshly ground black pepper

1 carrot, peeled and cut into 1-inch pieces

1 medium yellow onion, cut into 1-inch pieces

1 fennel bulb, cut into 1-inch pieces

Extra-virgin olive oil

1 bay leaf

2 fresh thyme sprigs

½ teaspoon whole black peppercorns

1 piece lemon peel, 1 inch wide and 3 inches long

½ cup dry white wine

4 cups organic chicken stock

FOR THE PIZZA

1 portion Basic Go-To Easy Pizza Dough (page 49)

2 tablespoons Essential Garlic Oil (page 69), plus more for finishing

¼ cup shredded part-skim mozzarella

1 cup arugula

1 (28-ounce) can whole San Marzano tomatoes, drained

Salt

Parmesan cheese

Freshly ground black pepper

1 recipe Tapenade (page 78)

TO MAKE THE BRAISE

1. Two days before you plan to serve the pizza, trim away the excess fat from the chicken legs and season them with salt and pepper. Cover and refrigerate overnight.

2. The next day, remove the chicken from the refrigerator and get ready to build the braise. Preheat the oven to 400°F. →

3. Sauté the carrot, onion, and fennel in a bit of olive oil until softened, about 5 minutes. Season with salt. Transfer to a cazuela large enough to hold the vegetables and chicken legs snugly in a single layer. Add the bay leaf, thyme, peppercorns, and lemon peel. Nestle in the chicken legs, skin-side down, then add the wine and enough stock to almost cover the meat. Cover tightly with aluminum foil and place in the oven.

4. After 15 minutes turn the oven down to 325°F. Cook for 30 minutes longer. Uncover the chicken, carefully turn the legs over so they're skin side up, and continue to cook until the meat is tender but not falling off the bone, about 20 minutes longer. The skin should be deeply browned and crispy.

5. Remove from the oven and let cool. Skim as much fat from the surface as possible. Discard the fat. Cover and refrigerate until ready to use.

6. The following day, remove the chicken from the refrigerator and allow it to come to room temperature. Shred the chicken meat from the bones. Chop the skin finely and mix it in with the meat. Strain the broth and use it for another purpose, such as soup. Discard the vegetables.

TO MAKE THE PIZZA

1. Following the directions for a fully prepped oven, make sure your fire is at the desired cooking temperature with a roiling flame and a brushed and cleaned oven floor. You are now ready to make a pizza.

2. Stretch out the dough as shown in "How to Shape a Pizza" (page 51). Lightly dust your pizza peel with flour. Place your stretched dough directly on the peel and proceed to build the pizza.

3. Brush the stretched dough with the garlic oil and spread the cheese evenly, leaving a ½-inch border all the way around the outside. Scatter the arugula over the entire pizza. Crush the tomatoes with your hands and arrange the chunky pieces on top, then fill in the spaces with the shredded chicken meat and skin. Sprinkle the entire pie with a pinch of salt.

4. Slide the pizza into the oven and bake for 3 to 5 minutes, rotating once or twice to ensure even cooking. Remove the pizza to a cutting board, grate Parmesan cheese over the pie, and add a few grinds of black pepper. Drizzle with tapenade.

5. Slice into 6 or 8 wedges. Brush the crust edges with a quick pass of the garlic oil to finish.

SUBSTITUTION TIP: *If you have a source for humanely raised organic rabbit, substitute bone-in skinless rabbit legs for the chicken.*

SHREDDED DUCK LEG AND WINTER SQUASH PIZZA WITH SCAMORZA

MAKES ONE 10-INCH PIZZA

Prep time: 20 minutes for the braise, 20 minutes for the pizza

Cook time: 1 hour 10 minutes for the braise, 3 to 5 minutes for the pizza

The headliner for this pizza is the unctuous duck leg, slowly braised, then shredded and crisped in the oven. The tender dark meat pairs seamlessly with a variety of seasonal winter squashes, and gets an added layer of smoke from the finish of Scamorza cheese. As with the previous pizza, which uses braised chicken legs, start two days before you plan to make this pizza: Season the duck legs on day one, braise them on day two, and build your pizza on day three.

FOR THE BRAISE

2 organic bone-in, skin-on whole duck legs

Salt

Freshly ground black pepper

1 carrot, peeled and cut into 1-inch pieces

1 leek, cut into 1-inch pieces

1 fennel bulb, cut into 1-inch pieces

Extra-virgin olive oil

1 bay leaf

2 fresh thyme sprigs

½ teaspoon whole black peppercorns

1 whole star anise

1 piece orange peel, 1 inch wide and 3 inches long

½ cup dry white wine

4 cups organic chicken stock

FOR THE PIZZA

½ winter squash, such as kabocha or butternut, peeled, seeded, and cut into ⅛-inch-thick slices

2 tablespoons Essential Garlic Oil (page 69), divided, plus more for finishing

Salt

1 portion Elevated Pizza Dough (page 52)

½ cup shredded Scamorza cheese

Parmesan cheese

Freshly ground black pepper

2 tablespoons chopped fresh parsley

TO MAKE THE BRAISE

1. Two days before you plan to serve the pizza, trim away the excess fat from the duck legs and season them with salt and pepper. Cover and refrigerate overnight.

2. The next day, remove the duck from the refrigerator and get ready to build the braise. Preheat the oven to 400°F. →

3. Sauté the carrot, leek, and fennel in a bit of olive oil until softened, about 5 minutes. Season with salt. Transfer to a cazuela large enough to hold the vegetables and duck legs snugly in a single layer. Add the bay leaf, thyme, peppercorns, star anise, and orange peel. Nestle in the duck legs, skin-side down, then add the wine and enough stock to almost cover the meat. Cover tightly with aluminum foil and place in the oven.

4. After 15 minutes turn the oven down to 325°F. Cook for 30 minutes longer. Uncover the duck, carefully turn the legs over so they're skin-side up, and continue to cook until the meat is tender but not falling off the bone, about 20 minutes longer. The skin should be deeply browned and crispy.

5. Remove from the oven and let cool. Skim as much fat from the surface as possible. Discard the fat. Cover and refrigerate until ready to use.

6. The following day, remove the duck from the refrigerator and allow it to come to room temperature. Shred the duck meat from the bones. Chop the skin finely and mix it in with the meat. Strain the broth and use it for another purpose such as soup. Discard the vegetables.

TO MAKE THE PIZZA

1. Toss the squash slices in 1 tablespoon of the garlic oil and season with salt. Arrange on a half sheet pan in a single layer and roast in a medium-hot oven until tender, 4 to 5 minutes. Allow the squash to cool before building the pie.

2. Following the directions for a fully prepped oven, make sure your fire is at the desired cooking temperature with a roiling flame and a brushed and cleaned oven floor. You are now ready to make a pizza.

3. Stretch out the dough as shown in "How to Shape a Pizza" (page 51). Lightly dust your pizza peel with flour. Place your stretched dough directly on the peel and proceed to build the pizza.

4. Brush the stretched dough with the remaining 1 tablespoon garlic oil and spread the shredded Scamorza evenly, leaving a ½-inch border all the way around the outside. Arrange the roasted squash slices in a single layer over the pie. Fill in the spaces with the shredded duck meat and skin. Sprinkle the entire pie with a pinch of salt.

5. Slide the pizza into the oven and bake for 3 to 5 minutes, rotating once or twice to ensure even cooking. Remove the pizza to a cutting board, grate Parmesan cheese over the entire pie, and add a few grinds of black pepper. Garnish with the chopped parsley. Slice into 6 or 8 wedges. Brush the crust edges with a quick pass of the garlic oil to finish.

PIZZA WITH FRESH FIGS, CARAMELIZED ONIONS, AND ANCHOIADE

MAKES ONE 10-INCH PIZZA

Prep time: 35 minutes
Cook time: 3 to 5 minutes

Salt-packed anchovies, fresh figs, fennel, and caramelized onions combine to create a uniquely flavored pizza that is reminiscent of a sunny afternoon in Provence. Pair this pie with the Farm Stand Vegetable Salad (page 218) and a bottle of chilled rosé and you will swear you can feel the Mediterranean trade winds blowing.

1 small yellow onion, thinly sliced
Extra-virgin olive oil
Salt
1 portion Basic Go-To Easy Pizza Dough
(page 49)
1 tablespoon Essential Garlic Oil
(page 69), plus more for finishing
½ cup Anchoiade (page 81)
1 fennel bulb, thinly sliced on a
mandoline
6 fresh ripe figs, such as black Mission,
stemmed and quartered
1 tablespoon chopped fresh thyme
Freshly ground black pepper

1. Toss the onion slices with olive oil and salt and place in a cazuela. Roast slowly in the mouth of the oven, tossing frequently. Prevent the onions from burning by adding a splash of water if needed. The onions will lose considerable volume, begin to color slightly, and become much sweeter. When the onions have deeply colored and lost most of their volume, after 20 minutes or so, remove the pan. Allow to cool.

2. Following the directions for a fully prepped oven, make sure your fire is at the desired cooking temperature with a roiling flame and a brushed and cleaned oven floor. You are now ready to make a pizza.

3. Stretch out the dough as shown in "How to Shape a Pizza" (page 51). Lightly dust your pizza peel with flour. Place your stretched dough directly on the peel and proceed to build the pizza. →

4. Brush the stretched dough with the garlic oil and spread the anchoiade evenly over the dough, leaving a ½-inch border all the way around the outside. Distribute the caramelized onions and sliced fennel over the pie, followed by the quartered figs. Sprinkle the entire pie with a pinch of salt and the chopped thyme.

5. Slide the pizza into the oven and bake for 3 to 5 minutes, rotating once or twice to ensure even cooking. Remove the pizza to a cutting board and add a few grinds of black pepper. Slice into 6 or 8 wedges. Brush the crust edges with a quick pass of the garlic oil to finish.

MOCK PISSALADIÈRE
ONION, ANCHOVY, AND NIÇOISE OLIVE PIZZA

MAKES ONE 10-INCH PIZZA
Prep time: 35 minutes
Cook time: 30 minutes

This niçoise recipe has all of the deliciousness of a true *pissaladière*, the classic savory tart from Provence. Traditionally, this dish is baked on flaky layers of puff pastry, or even a dough that requires longer cooking. You can forgo that preparation in favor of this quick wood-fired version.

½ cup extra-virgin olive oil

4 cups sliced yellow onion

Salt

2 tablespoons finely chopped fresh thyme

1 portion Elevated Pizza Dough (page 52)

2 tablespoons Essential Garlic Oil
    (page 69), plus more for finishing

10 salt-packed anchovies, rinsed, soaked,
    filleted (see Prep Tip), and halved
    lengthwise (40 pieces total)

½ cup pitted, halved niçoise olives

Freshly ground black pepper

1. Heat a wide-mouthed pan with a tight-fitting lid over high heat, add the olive oil and then the onions, and season with a generous teaspoon of salt. Stir to coat the onions in the oil and then cover the pot. Cook over high heat for 5 minutes, uncovering and stirring occasionally to prevent scorching.

2. After 5 minutes, or when the onions begin to soften in their own juice, uncover the pot and turn the heat down to medium-low. Cook the onions for 20 minutes, stirring occasionally and adding a splash of water if they start to color. Stir in the chopped thyme, then spread the cooked onions in a single layer on a half sheet to facilitate cooling.

3. Following the directions for a fully prepped oven, make sure your fire is at the desired cooking temperature with a roiling flame and a brushed and cleaned oven floor. You are now ready to make a pizza.

4. Stretch out the dough as shown in "How to Shape a Pizza" (page 51). Lightly dust your pizza peel with flour. Place your stretched dough directly on the peel and proceed to build the pizza. →

5. Brush the stretched dough with the garlic oil. Spread the cooled onions over the dough, leaving a ½-inch border. Arrange the sliced anchovy fillets in a diamond pattern and place an olive half in the "window" of each diamond.

6. Slide the pizza into the oven and bake for 3 to 5 minutes, rotating once or twice to ensure even cooking. Remove the pizza to a cutting board and add a few grinds of black pepper. Slice into 6 or 8 wedges. Brush the crust edges with a quick pass of the garlic oil to finish.

PREP TIP: *To prepare the anchovies, first rinse off the excess salt. Place the anchovies in a small bowl, cover with cool water, and allow to stand for 10 minutes. Each anchovy has two fillets; separate the fillets from the backbone by gently peeling back the flesh under slowly running water. Remove and discard the dorsal fin and tail. Blot the fillets dry with a paper towel.*

WHIPPED SALT COD AND POTATO PIZZA

MAKES ONE 10-INCH PIZZA

Prep time: 30 minutes for the salt cod, 15 minutes for the pizza

Cook time: 20 minutes for the salt cod, 5 minutes for the pizza

Cod may have been the fish that saved the world—through salting and drying, the shelf life of this once plentiful fish became indefinite. A source of protein that was light and shelf stable meant it could feed explorers sent to sea and entire villages through the lean winter months. As a result, salted cod appears frequently in dishes from western Europe to Scandinavia. Here we blend the poached fish with potatoes, garlic, and olive oil, pair it with the incendiary harissa sauce, and top it with a perfectly baked egg.

FOR THE WHIPPED SALT COD

1 pound salt cod

1 pound Yellow Finn or russet potatoes, peeled and quartered

2 cups water

2 cups whole milk

½ yellow onion, quartered

1 whole garlic clove, peeled

1 bay leaf

1 fresh thyme sprig

¾ cup extra-virgin olive oil

2 tablespoons garlic, pounded in a mortar and pestle

Salt

FOR THE PIZZA

8 ounces Yellow Finn potatoes, sliced ⅛ inch thick

Salt

Extra-virgin olive oil

1 portion Basic Go-To Easy Pizza Dough (page 49)

½ cup Harissa (page 80)

1 egg

Freshly ground black pepper →

TO MAKE THE WHIPPED SALT COD

1. The day before you plan to make this pizza, place the salt cod in a large bowl and cover with water. Soak in the refrigerator, replacing the water several times throughout the soaking process.

2. The next day, cook the potatoes in boiling salted water until easily pierced with the tip of a knife, about 10 minutes. Drain well, return to the warm pan, and allow to dry out until cool.

3. Drain the salt cod. In a large pot, combine the salt cod, water, milk, onion, whole garlic clove, bay leaf, and thyme. Cut a round of parchment paper large enough to fit over the pot and press it down on the fish. Make a slight tear in the paper to allow steam to escape.

4. Slowly bring the pot to a simmer over medium heat, then turn the heat down to a bare simmer and poach the fish until tender, 8 to 10 minutes. Lift the fish from the poaching liquid and cool slightly. Reserve ½ cup of the poaching liquid. Pick over the fish, removing any dark spots or bones. Transfer the fish to the bowl of an electric stand mixer fitted with the paddle attachment.

5. Warm the olive oil and pounded garlic over low heat until it begins to sizzle and immediately remove from the heat, being careful to not allow the garlic to color.

6. Gradually beat the cooked potatoes into the fish, moistening with a few drops of the reserved poaching liquid. Add the warm garlic oil and continue beating. Taste for seasoning—it may need salt, believe it or not. The mixture should be smooth and highly seasoned, and absorb the oil and poaching liquid. Set aside until ready to use (or cover and refrigerate if not using until the following day).

TO MAKE THE PIZZA

1. In a bowl, toss the sliced potatoes with a generous pinch of salt and moisten with a splash each of olive oil and water. Arrange the potatoes in a single layer on an unlined half sheet and roast in a very hot oven until they begin to take on color and soften, 4 to 7 minutes. Allow the potatoes to cool completely, taste, and adjust the seasoning with more salt if needed. Set aside until you're ready to build the pizza.

2. Following the directions for a fully prepped oven, make sure your fire is at the desired cooking temperature with a roiling flame and a brushed and cleaned oven floor. You are now ready to make a pizza.

3. Stretch out the dough as shown in "How to Shape a Pizza" (page 51). Lightly dust your pizza peel with flour. Place your stretched dough directly on the peel and proceed to build the pizza.

4. Brush the stretched dough evenly with the harissa, leaving a ½-inch border all the way around the outside. Next, layer the cooked potato slices, followed by small spoonfuls of the whipped salt cod.

5. Carefully crack the egg into a small bowl. Discard the watery layer that surrounds the white, taking care to keep the yolk intact.

6. Slide the pizza into the oven and bake for 2 minutes to set the bottom of the crust. Remove the pie, carefully tip the egg onto the center of the pizza, and return it to the oven. Bake until the egg white is opaque but the yolk is still runny, another 2 to 3 minutes. Remove the pizza to a cutting board and add a few grinds of black pepper. Slice into 6 or 8 wedges.

PREP TIP: *Ask for salt cod at your local fish market or find it at better ethnic grocery stores. Start a day before you plan to make your pizza, as the cod needs to soak in several changes of water to soften before cooking.*

FLATBREAD OF SMOKED SALMON AND CAVIAR

MAKES ONE 10-INCH PIZZA
Prep time: 15 minutes
Cook time: 3 to 5 minutes

When I sat down to compile a list of recipes for this book, one of the first pizzas that came to mind was the dish celebrity chef Wolfgang Puck created at his legendary restaurant, Spago, in 1982. No one had ever thought to put smoked salmon on wood-fired pizza before, but millions are glad he did—myself included. If there ever was a time to pair a glass of Champagne or sparkling wine with pizza, this is it.

1 portion North African Flatbread dough (page 60)

¼ cup thinly sliced red onion, soaked in ice water for 10 minutes

½ cup Wild Fennel Sauce (page 77)

4 ounces high-quality smoked salmon

¼ cup crème fraîche

1 ounce caviar or salmon roe (optional)

2 tablespoons finely chopped fresh chives

Freshly ground black pepper

1. Following the directions for a fully prepped oven, make sure your fire is at the desired cooking temperature with a roiling flame and a brushed and cleaned oven floor. You are now ready to make a pizza.

2. Stretch out the dough as shown in "How to Shape a Pizza" (page 51). Lightly dust your pizza peel with flour. Place your stretched dough directly on the peel and proceed to build the pizza.

3. Drain the onions from the ice water and dry thoroughly.

4. Brush the stretched dough with the fennel sauce, spreading evenly. Leave a ½-inch border around the outside of the dough. Slide the dough into the oven and bake for 3 to 5 minutes, rotating once or twice to ensure even cooking.

5. Remove the flatbread to a cutting board, and drape the smoked salmon slices over the pie. Garnish with the red onion. Drizzle over the crème fraîche, distribute the caviar or salmon roe evenly, if using, and garnish with the chopped chives. Slice into 6 or 8 wedges. Add a few grinds of black pepper.

ROASTED CLAM AND BACON PIZZA

MAKES ONE 10-INCH PIZZA
Prep time: 30 minutes
Cook time: 3 to 5 minutes

When I order a platter of fresh clams, either raw or steamed, it seems as though I taste all the flavors of the sea. Each clam is an individually wrapped maritime gift. Add crumbled smoked bacon to this briny pizza, top it with a refreshing parsley and mint salad, and squeeze a lemon over the entire pie.

1 pound littleneck or cherrystone clams

¼ cup dry white wine

Extra-virgin olive oil

1 portion Elevated Pizza Dough (page 52)

2 tablespoons Essential Garlic Oil (page 69), plus more for finishing

¼ cup Wild Fennel Sauce (page 77)

½ cup sliced fennel bulb, dressed with olive oil and salt

8 ounces smoked bacon, cooked until crispy and crumbled

2 tablespoons heavy cream

Salt

¼ cup chopped fresh flat-leaf parsley

10 mint leaves, torn into bite-size pieces

1 lemon

Freshly ground black pepper

1. Following the directions for a fully prepped oven, make sure your fire is at the desired cooking temperature with a roiling flame and a brushed and cleaned oven floor.

2. Wash the clams thoroughly in a bowl of cold water, removing as much sandy grit as possible. Transfer the clams to a cazuela large enough for them to fit in a single layer, add the white wine, and drizzle with olive oil. Roast in the hottest part of the oven until the clams begin to open. Remove any clams as they open and return the cazuela to the oven to finish cooking the rest. Repeat until all the clams have opened. Discard any that remain closed. When cool enough to handle, strain the liquid from the cazuela into a small bowl and pull the clams from their shells, adding them to the roasting liquid as you go to keep them moist.

3. Stretch out the dough as shown in "How to Shape a Pizza" (page 51). Lightly dust your pizza peel with flour. Place your stretched dough directly on the peel and proceed to build the pizza.

4. Brush the stretched dough with the garlic oil and spread the fennel sauce evenly, leaving a ½-inch border all the way around the outside. Arrange the sliced fennel and the clams over the pie. Scatter the crumbled bacon on top. Drizzle with the cream. Sprinkle the entire pie with a pinch of salt.

5. Slide the pizza into the oven and bake for 3 to 5 minutes, rotating once or twice to ensure even cooking. Remove the pizza to a cutting board. In a small bowl, toss together the parsley and mint. Dress with olive oil and salt and scatter over the pie. Give a big squeeze of lemon juice over the entire pizza and add a few grinds of black pepper. Slice into 6 or 8 wedges. Brush the crust edges with a quick pass of the garlic oil to finish.

SQUID PIZZA WITH CHERRY TOMATOES AND AIOLI

MAKES ONE 10-INCH PIZZA

Prep time: 30 minutes
Cook time: 3 to 5 minutes

Squid roasted in the wood oven is a revelation. It captures the wood smoke perfectly and cooks up quickly, which keeps it tender. Don't be intimidated by handling and cleaning fresh squid; it is quick work and well worth it. Choose your squid carefully. The eyes should be clear, the flesh firm to the touch, and the skin intact. The skin of fresh squid is creamy in color, with reddish-brown spots. As squid ages, the skin turns pinkish.

1 portion Basic Go-To Easy Pizza Dough (page 49)

2 tablespoons Essential Garlic Oil (page 69), plus more for finishing

½ cup Wild Fennel Sauce (page 77)

1 cup arugula, packed tightly

1 cup halved cherry tomatoes, dressed with olive oil and salt

8 ounces fresh squid, cleaned and cut into rings and tentacles, dressed with olive oil and salt

¼ cup fresh basil leaves

Salt

1 recipe Aïoli (page 79)

1. Following the directions for a fully prepped oven, make sure your fire is at the desired cooking temperature with a roiling flame and a brushed and cleaned oven floor. You are now ready to make a pizza.

2. Stretch out the dough as shown in "How to Shape a Pizza" (page 51). Lightly dust your pizza peel with flour. Place your stretched dough directly on the peel and proceed to build the pizza.

3. Brush the stretched dough with the garlic oil and spread the fennel sauce evenly, leaving a ½-inch border all the way around the outside. Arrange the arugula, cherry tomatoes, and squid rings and tentacles. Garnish with the whole basil leaves, pressing lightly into the sauce. Season the entire pie with a pinch of salt.

4. Slide the pizza into the oven and bake for 3 to 5 minutes, rotating once or twice to ensure even cooking. Remove the pizza to a cutting board.

5. Thin the aïoli with a few drops of water or lemon juice to achieve a thick, pourable sauce. Drizzle liberally over the pie. Slice into 6 or 8 wedges. Brush the crust edges with a quick pass of the garlic oil to finish.

PREP TIP: *To clean a squid, lay the squid out in front of you on a cutting board, left to right. Slice just below the eye and pull away the tentacle portion. Feel for the tiny hard beak within the tentacles and discard it. Reserve the tentacles in a bowl set over ice. With the back of the knife, exert even pressure and slide down the body of the squid, pressing out the internal organs and ink sac. Discard them. Repeat until the squid is empty. Reach inside the cavity and remove the long, clear cartilage and discard. Slice the body into half-inch rings and add to the tentacles over ice.*

SHRIMP, SWEET PEPPER, AND CHERRY TOMATO PIZZA WITH GREEN GARLIC

MAKES ONE 10-INCH PIZZA
Prep time: 30 minutes
Cook time: 3 to 5 minutes

When the cavalcade of summer produce is in full force, I like to create combinations that marry seafood, faraway spices, and local vegetables. Any sweet peppers will do in this recipe. However, I urge you to explore the full range of shapes and colors available, or add a single hot pepper to the mix for a surprise tang. Marash pepper flakes come from Turkey and have an earthy, fruity flavor. If your local store doesn't carry them, you can find them online.

1 cup Jimmy Nardello peppers, or a mix of sweet and hot peppers

Extra-virgin olive oil

Salt

1 portion Whole-Wheat Pizza Dough (page 56) or Spelt Pizza Dough (page 54)

1 tablespoon Essential Garlic Oil (page 69), plus more for finishing

2 tablespoons finely chopped green garlic (optional)

½ cup halved cherry tomatoes, seasoned with olive oil and salt

12 medium shrimp, peeled, deveined, and halved lengthwise

¼ cup fresh green or purple basil leaves

1 teaspoon Marash pepper flakes (optional)

1. Remove the seeds and stems from the peppers, thinly slice, and dress them with olive oil and salt. Let them macerate for 10 minutes before you begin to make your pizza.

2. Following the directions for a fully prepped oven, make sure your fire is at the desired cooking temperature with a roiling flame and a brushed and cleaned oven floor. You are now ready to make a pizza.

3. Stretch out the dough as shown in "How to Shape a Pizza" (page 51). Lightly dust your pizza peel with flour. Place your stretched dough directly on the peel and proceed to build the pizza.

4. Brush the stretched dough with the garlic oil and scatter the peppers and green garlic (if using) evenly, leaving a ½-inch border all the way around the outside. Arrange the cherry tomatoes, shrimp, and basil over the pie. Sprinkle the entire pie with a pinch of salt. Garnish with the Marash pepper flakes, if using.

5. Slide the pizza into the oven and bake for 3 to 5 minutes, rotating once or twice to ensure even cooking. Remove the pizza to a cutting board and slice into 6 or 8 wedges. Brush the crust edges with a quick pass of the garlic oil to finish.

A CLOSER LOOK: *Jimmy Nardello peppers are popular in Northern California for their sweet flavor and attractive appearance, and also because they are easy to grow. Long, twisted, wrinkly, and ranging from green to candy apple red, they give the impression they are fiery but are far from it. I will leave the origins of the name to those who fancy themselves culinary detectives.*

7 VEGETABLE PIZZAS

AS SATISFYING AS A PERFECTLY EXECUTED meat-topped pizza can be, it perhaps can't touch the heights of a garden-fresh pie. That may be heresy to some, but if you consider all the four seasons have to offer, and add to that the kingdom of earthy mushrooms . . . well, the combinations are limitless.

The adaptability of every class of vegetable to complement pizza says one of two things: Either a blistery pie, fresh from a fiery oven, supersedes the toppings; or the introduction of seasonal vegetables and mushrooms to the wood oven elevates them beyond reproach. This debate—like our fire—rages on.

These vegetable-topped offerings are mere suggestions that I've found to be particularly tasty, yet they only begin to scratch the surface of possible combinations. Create your own playlist of vegetable pizzas. Let your garden dictate dinner, and I guarantee you'll be planting next summer's harvest with intentions of re-creating tonight's menu.

PIZZA MARGHERITA

MAKES ONE 10-INCH PIZZA
Prep time: 10 minutes
Cook time: 3 to 5 minutes

The simple Margherita pizza is on every trattoria menu for a reason. When done correctly, this ubiquitous Italian staple highlights fresh ingredients at their peak of flavor. Whatever the origins of the name (honoring a queen, is one theory), just remember the colors of the Italian *bandiera*—red, white, and green—and you will always have the recipe at hand.

1 portion Basic Go-To Easy Pizza Dough
(page 49)
1 tablespoon Essential Garlic Oil
(page 69), plus more for finishing
½ cup Simple Tomato Sauce (page 70)
½ cup shredded part-skim mozzarella
or 4 ounces buffalo mozzarella,
thinly sliced
8 fresh basil leaves
Salt
Parmesan cheese
Freshly ground black pepper

1. Following the directions for a fully prepped oven, make sure your fire is at the desired cooking temperature with a roiling flame and a brushed and cleaned oven floor. You are now ready to make a pizza.

2. Stretch out the dough as shown in "How to Shape a Pizza" (page 51). Lightly dust your pizza peel with flour. Place your stretched dough directly on the peel and proceed to build the pizza.

3. Brush the stretched dough with the garlic oil and spread the tomato sauce evenly over the dough, leaving a ½-inch border all the way around the outside. Arrange the shredded or sliced cheese, whichever you prefer, distributing evenly. Garnish the dressed pie with the basil leaves, pressing lightly into the sauce and cheese. Season the entire pie with a pinch of salt.

4. Slide the pizza into the oven and bake for 3 to 5 minutes, rotating once or twice to ensure even cooking. Remove the pizza to a cutting board, grate Parmesan cheese over the entire pie, and add a few grinds of black pepper. Slice into 6 or 8 wedges. Brush the crust edges with a quick pass of the garlic oil to finish.

GLUTEN-FREE PESTO PIZZA

MAKES ONE 9-BY-13-INCH PIZZA

Prep time: 30 minutes
Cook time: about 10 minutes

Since the gluten-free pizza dough must be prebaked, it makes sense to use toppings that do not require a long time in the oven. Basil pesto, summer squash, sweet corn, and cherry tomatoes are punctuated by tangy goat cheese for a delicious taste of summer in every bite of this pizza.

1 cup fresh sweet corn kernels

Extra-virgin olive oil

Salt

1 portion Gluten-Free Pizza Dough (page 58), prebaked

4 tablespoons Essential Garlic Oil (page 69), divided, plus more for finishing

¾ cup Basic Pesto (page 74)

1 cup thinly sliced yellow summer squash

1 cup halved cherry tomatoes

2 ounces goat cheese, crumbled

Freshly ground black pepper

Parmesan cheese

1. Toss the fresh corn kernels with olive oil and salt and transfer to a cazuela large enough to hold the corn in a single shallow layer. Roast in the wood oven for 4 to 6 minutes, tossing once to prevent scorching. Remove from the oven and allow to cool before building the pizza.

2. Following the directions for a fully prepped oven, make sure your fire is at the desired cooking temperature with a roiling flame and a brushed and cleaned oven floor. You are now ready to make a pizza.

3. Prebake the gluten-free dough, as described in the recipe (page 58). Remove the cooled dough from the quarter sheet pan and build the pizza directly on the wooden peel.

4. Brush the stretched dough with 2 tablespoons of the garlic oil and spread the pesto evenly over the dough, leaving a ½-inch border all the way around the outside. In a separate bowl, toss the squash slices with a splash of olive oil and season with a generous pinch of salt. Arrange the slices in a thin layer over the sauce. Mix the roasted corn and the cherry tomatoes together, adjust the seasoning, and scatter over the pizza. Dot the pie with the goat cheese and drizzle the entire pizza with the remaining 2 tablespoons garlic oil.

5. Slide the pizza into the oven long enough to warm the pizza toppings through and finish cooking the gluten-free dough, about 3 minutes.

6. Remove from the oven and add a few grinds of black pepper. Grate the Parmesan cheese over the pie. Slice into 10 rectangles. Brush the crust edges with a quick pass of the garlic oil to finish.

PIZZA WITH FRESH TOMATOES, GYPSY PEPPERS, AND CAPERS

MAKES ONE 10-INCH PIZZA

Prep time: 30 minutes
Cook time: 3 to 5 minutes

Choose a colorful array of tomatoes for this pizza, and be sure to use your sharpest knife to cut them into even, thin slices. Visit your local farmers' market and sample what the growers are bringing in; mix and match colors for a real showstopper. The same goes for the sweet gypsy peppers: Buy a colorful mix and remove the seeds before slicing them paper thin on the mandoline. Seek out the imported capers that are dry-packed in salt, not brine; that pickled note would not be welcome here.

1 tablespoon salt-packed capers, rinsed

1 portion Basic Go-To Easy Pizza Dough (page 49)

2 tablespoons Essential Garlic Oil (page 69), plus more for dressing and finishing

¼ cup Oven-Roasted Red Sauce (page 71)

8 ounces ripe organic heirloom tomatoes, very thinly sliced and drained

Salt

½ cup shredded part-skim mozzarella

½ cup seeded and very thinly sliced gypsy peppers

2 tablespoons roughly chopped fresh marjoram or oregano

1. Put the capers in a small bowl and cover with water. Set aside and allow to soak for 10 minutes. Lift the capers from the water and drain on a paper towel, then roughly chop and set aside until ready to use.

2. Following the directions for a fully prepped oven, make sure your fire is at the desired cooking temperature with a roiling flame and a brushed and cleaned oven floor. You are now ready to make a pizza.

3. Stretch out the dough as shown in "How to Shape a Pizza" (page 51). Lightly dust your pizza peel with flour. Place your stretched dough directly on the peel and proceed to build the pizza.

4. Brush the dough with the garlic oil and spoon over the red sauce in a few random streaks. Arrange the drained tomatoes, taking care not to overlap the slices. Season the tomato slices with a good pinch or two of salt. Then evenly top with the shredded cheese.

5. In a small bowl, toss the sliced peppers with a good pinch of salt and a splash of garlic oil. Scatter the dressed peppers over the pie.

6. Slide the pizza into the oven and bake for 3 to 5 minutes, rotating once or twice to ensure even cooking. Remove the pizza to a cutting board and slice into 6 or 8 wedges. Garnish with the chopped capers and marjoram. Brush the crust edges with a quick pass of the garlic oil to finish.

SUBSTITUTION TIP: *If you can't find salt-packed capers, use capers packed in brine. Soak the brined capers for 20 minutes before draining and chopping.*

ASPARAGUS AND FAVA BEAN PIZZA WITH TAPENADE

MAKES ONE 10-INCH PIZZA
Prep time: 30 minutes
Cook time: 3 to 5 minutes

When spring vegetables have begun in earnest, keep an eye out for the first fava beans of the season. They're sweet, tender, and slightly nutty, with what can only be described as a taste like the color green looks. Fava beans need to be shelled from their pithy pods, and then the tough outer skins removed by blanching. Avoid using favas later in their season for this recipe, because the larger beans tend to be starchy and tough.

3 thick asparagus spears

Extra-virgin olive oil

Salt

1 portion Whole-Wheat Pizza Dough (page 56) or Spelt Pizza Dough (page 54)

2 tablespoons Essential Garlic Oil (page 69), plus more for finishing

½ cup Tapenade (page 78)

1 cup fava beans, shelled and blanched (see Prep Tip)

2 ounces fresh ricotta cheese

Parmesan cheese

Freshly ground black pepper

2 tablespoons fresh mint leaves, torn into bite-size pieces

1. Prepare the asparagus by snapping off the woody stems and discarding. Using a mandoline, carefully slice the raw asparagus lengthwise, creating paper-thin ribbons. Toss the asparagus ribbons in a small bowl with a splash of olive oil and a pinch of salt.

2. Following the directions for a fully prepped oven, make sure your fire is at the desired cooking temperature with a roiling flame and a brushed and cleaned oven floor. You are now ready to make a pizza.

3. Stretch out the dough as shown in "How to Shape a Pizza" (page 51). Lightly dust your pizza peel with flour. Place your stretched dough directly on the peel and proceed to build the pizza.

4. Brush the stretched dough with the garlic oil and spread the tapenade evenly over the dough, leaving a ½-inch border all the way around the outside. Arrange the dressed asparagus ribbons over the dough, followed by the prepared fava beans. Dollop small spoonfuls of the ricotta around the pie. Season the pie with a pinch of salt.

5. Slide the pizza into the oven and bake for 3 to 5 minutes, rotating once or twice to ensure even cooking. Remove the pizza to a cutting board, grate the Parmesan cheese over the entire pie, and add a few grinds of black pepper. Sprinkle the entire pizza with the chopped mint. Slice into 6 or 8 wedges. Brush the crust edges with a quick pass of the garlic oil to finish.

PREP TIP: *Shell the favas by breaking open the pods along the seam and pulling out the beans. While you're doing this, bring a small pot of water to a boil. Have a bowl filled with ice water ready to stop the beans from overcooking. Blanch the beans for 30 to 45 seconds, remove, and plunge into the ice bath. Drain and separate the inner beans from their tough outer skins.*

EGGPLANT PIZZA WITH FRESH MOZZARELLA AND OVEN-DRIED HERBS

MAKES ONE 10-INCH PIZZA

Prep time: 40 minutes

Cook time: 3 to 5 minutes

Dried herbs give a different dimension to cooked foods, much deeper in flavor than their fresh former selves. For that reason, I like to cook with dried herbs and finish dishes with fresh. In this recipe, I marinate sliced eggplant with dried herbs, then flash-bake them before assembling the pizza. It only makes sense to use the Oven-Roasted Red Sauce on this pie, since deep flavors are at play.

1 medium globe eggplant

1 teaspoon salt

¼ cup plus 1 tablespoon extra-virgin olive oil, divided

2 teaspoons mixed oven-dried herbs, such as oregano or marjoram (see Prep Tip)

1 portion Elevated Pizza Dough (page 52)

2 tablespoons Essential Garlic Oil (page 69), plus more for finishing

½ cup Oven-Roasted Red Sauce (page 71)

4 ounces buffalo mozzarella, thinly sliced

Salt

Freshly ground black pepper

Parmesan cheese

1. Use a vegetable peeler to peel some of the skin from the eggplant in a striped pattern. The skin can cook up tough, but a little toughness is fine. Slice into ⅛-inch-thick rounds and season with the salt, ¼ cup of olive oil, and the oven-dried herbs. Toss well to combine. Oil a half sheet pan with the remaining 1 tablespoon of olive oil and arrange the eggplant in a single layer. Roast in the window of the wood oven for 4 to 5 minutes to soften the eggplant; rotate as needed to avoid burning the slices. Allow to cool before building the pizza.

2. Following the directions for a fully prepped oven, make sure your fire is at the desired cooking temperature with a roiling flame and a brushed and cleaned oven floor. You are now ready to make a pizza.

3. Stretch out the dough as shown in "How to Shape a Pizza" (page 51). Lightly dust your pizza peel with flour. Place your stretched dough directly on the peel and proceed to build the pizza.

4. Brush the stretched dough with the garlic oil and spread the red sauce evenly over the dough, leaving a ½-inch border all the way around the outside. Arrange the eggplant slices in a thin layer over the sauce. Layer on the mozzarella. Season the entire pie with a pinch of salt.

5. Slide the pizza into the oven and bake for 3 to 5 minutes, rotating once or twice to ensure even cooking. Remove the pizza to a cutting board and add a few grinds of black pepper. Grate the Parmesan cheese over the entire pizza. Slice into 6 or 8 wedges. Brush the crust edges with a quick pass of the garlic oil to finish.

PREP TIP: *Fresh herbs are easy to grow at home in window boxes, flowerpots, or neglected corners of the yard. Harvest them and make a large batch of dried herbs using the residual heat of a long-expired fire. Arrange the herb sprigs in a single layer on a half sheet pan and place in the mouth of the oven. Dry the herbs slowly overnight. I'm fond of rosemary, oregano, marjoram, and sage for this treatment. Stored in an airtight glass jar, they will keep almost indefinitely.*

WHOLE-WHEAT PIZZA WITH GREENS, RAPINI, PINE NUTS, AND RICOTTA SALATA

MAKES ONE 10-INCH PIZZA
Prep time: 40 minutes
Cook time: about 10 minutes

Eating a slice of this pie feels as if you are getting healthier by the bite. Rapini, also known as broccoli rabe, adds a sharp, tasty bite along with many vitamins. Choose your favorite dark, leafy greens such as chard, kale, or spinach. Aged ricotta, known as ricotta salata, is unlike fresh ricotta; it is wonderfully dry and dense with a good salt kick. Grate it over the pizza after it comes out of the oven.

8 ounces Swiss chard, Lacinato kale, or spinach
¼ cup chopped rapini
1 tablespoon extra-virgin olive oil
Salt
1 portion Whole-Wheat Pizza Dough (page 56)
1 tablespoon Essential Garlic Oil (page 69), plus more for finishing
½ cup Salsa Bianca (page 75)
2 ounces ricotta salata, grated
4 fresh nasturtium flowers, petals only (optional)
Freshly ground black pepper

1. First, precook the two main vegetables that top this pizza. Blanch the greens in salted boiling water, drain thoroughly, squeeze out any excess moisture, and chop. Sauté the chopped rapini in a covered pan in 1 tablespoon of olive oil, a splash of water, and a pinch of salt. Cook for 3 to 5 minutes. Allow to cool before building the pizza.

2. Following the directions for a fully prepped oven, make sure your fire is at the desired cooking temperature with a roiling flame and a brushed and cleaned oven floor. You are now ready to make a pizza.

3. Stretch out the dough as shown in "How to Shape a Pizza" (page 51). Lightly dust your pizza peel with flour. Place your stretched dough directly on the peel and proceed to build the pizza.

4. Brush the stretched dough with the garlic oil and spread the salsa bianca evenly over the dough, leaving a ½-inch border all the way around the outside. Arrange the greens and rapini in a thin layer over the sauce. Take care not to overcrowd the pizza. Season the entire pie with a pinch of salt.

5. Slide the pizza into the oven and bake for 3 to 5 minutes, rotating once or twice to ensure even cooking. Remove the pizza to a cutting board. Garnish with grated ricotta salata, and scatter the flower petals about, if using. Add a few grinds of black pepper. Slice into 6 or 8 wedges. Brush the crust edges with a quick pass of the garlic oil to finish.

SUBSTITUTION TIP: *If you can't find ricotta salata, use fresh ricotta or even wide shards of Parmesan cheese in its place. If you're using fresh ricotta, bake it on the pie rather than adding it after the pizza is done.*

SQUASH AND SQUASH BLOSSOM PIZZA WITH CHERRY TOMATOES

MAKES ONE 10-INCH PIZZA
Prep time: 20 minutes
Cook time: 3 to 5 minutes

1 portion Basic Go-To Easy Pizza Dough (page 49)

1 tablespoon Essential Garlic Oil (page 69), plus more for finishing

½ cup Salsa Bianca (page 75)

½ cup thinly sliced yellow summer squash

3 fresh squash blossoms, stems and pistils removed, torn into 3-inch-wide ribbons

½ cup halved cherry tomatoes

Salt

Parmesan cheese

Freshly ground black pepper

What would summer be without an assortment of squashes and zucchinis? Put a dent in your bumper crop with this vibrantly colored and delicious pizza. Squash blossoms reinforce the core flavors while lending a complementary note with their elegant orange petals. Cherry tomatoes, both sweet and acidic, act as rays of harnessed sunshine and expertly balance the unctuous Salsa Bianca. Harvest the male blossoms and leave the females to produce more squashes throughout the growing season. How can you tell the difference? The female blossoms have a zucchini attached. The males are just a flower on a stem.

1. Following the directions for a fully prepped oven, make sure your fire is at the desired cooking temperature with a roiling flame and a brushed and cleaned oven floor. You are now ready to make a pizza.

2. Stretch out the dough as shown in "How to Shape a Pizza" (page 51). Lightly dust your pizza peel with flour. Place your stretched dough directly on the peel and proceed to build the pizza.

3. Brush the stretched dough with the garlic oil and spread the salsa bianca evenly over the dough, leaving a ½-inch border all the way around the outside.

Arrange the slices of yellow squash so they don't overlap one another, fill in the spaces with the torn squash blossoms, and, finally, scatter the halved cherry tomatoes. Sprinkle the entire pie with a pinch of salt.

4. Slide the pizza into the oven and bake for 3 to 5 minutes, rotating once or twice to ensure even cooking. Remove the pizza to a cutting board, grate Parmesan cheese over the entire pie, and add a few grinds of black pepper. Slice into 6 or 8 wedges. Brush the crust edges with a quick pass of the garlic oil to finish.

ARTICHOKES, LEEKS, AND GREMOLATA PIZZA

MAKES ONE 10-INCH PIZZA
Prep time: 30 minutes
Cook time: about 10 minutes

This pie demands a gentle hand when it comes to saucing. Ideally, you want to taste the freshness of the artichokes, the sweetness of the leeks, and the slightly sharp accent of the gremolata. Instead of spreading the entire dough with the red sauce, paint it with a streak here and there for a hint of acidity.

1 large leek

1 tablespoon olive oil, plus more for dressing

Salt

1 portion Whole-Wheat Pizza Dough (page 56) or Spelt Pizza Dough (page 54)

1 tablespoon Essential Garlic Oil (page 69), plus more for finishing

¼ cup Simple Tomato Sauce (page 70)

2 ounces fresh ricotta

½ cup baby artichokes, outer leaves removed

2 tablespoons gremolata (see A Closer Look)

1. Begin by peeling away the outer layer of the leek. Trim and discard the root end and the tough upper green portion. Cut in half lengthwise, then crosswise into ¼-inch-thick slices. Rinse in a bowl of water if there is any grit in between the layers. Drain and toss the leek in 1 tablespoon of olive oil, then season with salt. Transfer to a cazuela large enough to hold the leeks in a single layer. Cook, stirring often, in a medium-hot section of the oven. Be careful to not let them burn, as they will become tough. Add a splash of water if the cazuela begins to dry out before the leeks are cooked through and soft, about 5 to 7 minutes. Remove from the oven and allow to cool before building the pizza.

2. Following the directions for a fully prepped oven, make sure your fire is at the desired cooking temperature with a roiling flame and a brushed and cleaned oven floor. You are now ready to make a pizza.

3. Stretch out the dough as shown in "How to Shape a Pizza" (page 51). Lightly dust your pizza peel with flour. Place your stretched dough directly on the peel and proceed to build the pizza.

4. Brush the stretched dough with the garlic oil and spread the tomato sauce lightly in streaks. Arrange the stewed leeks evenly over the sauce, and add small spoonfuls of the ricotta around the pie. Season the pie with a pinch of salt. Quickly slice the artichokes as thinly as possible on a mandoline and place in a small bowl. Season with a few drops of olive oil and salt to inhibit burning while in the oven. Scatter evenly over the pizza.

5. Slide the pizza into the oven and bake for 3 to 5 minutes, rotating once or twice to ensure even cooking. Remove the pizza to a cutting board and slice into 6 or 8 wedges. Garnish generously with the gremolata. Brush the crust edges with a quick pass of the garlic oil to finish.

A CLOSER LOOK: *Gremolata is a fancy name for a trio of parsley, garlic, and lemon zest, chopped individually to the same consistency and then mixed together. Simply combine 2 tablespoons finely chopped fresh flat-leaf parsley, 1 minced garlic clove, and the zest of 1 lemon. You will find that the sum is greater than the parts.*

ARTICHOKE PIZZA WITH ROASTED RED ONIONS AND FRESH THYME

MAKES ONE 10-INCH PIZZA
Prep time: 20 minutes
Cook time: about 15 minutes

Artichokes are one of those vegetables that often get overlooked, perhaps because many people have the idea that they require a great deal of preparation. Not so. Here they top the pie raw and emerge nutty and slightly crisped. Look for small artichokes that are tightly packed with leaves and do not yield to gentle pressure.

1 medium sweet red onion, cut crosswise into ½-inch-thick slices

Salt

2 tablespoons Essential Garlic Oil (page 69), divided, plus more for finishing

1 portion Basic Go-To Easy Pizza Dough (page 49)

¼ cup Salsa Bianca (page 75)

½ cup shredded part-skim mozzarella

½ cup baby artichokes, outer leaves removed

Extra-virgin olive oil

1 tablespoon chopped fresh thyme

1. Season the onion slices with salt and brush both sides with 1 tablespoon of garlic oil, trying to keep the rings intact. Arrange in a single layer on a half sheet and roast slowly in the window of the oven until the onion slices soften, caramelize, and char slightly, about 10 minutes. Rotate the sheet pan often for even cooking and turn the slices over if they begin to color too strongly on the bottom. Allow to cool before building the pizza.

2. Following the directions for a fully prepped oven, make sure your fire is at the desired cooking temperature with a roiling flame and a brushed and cleaned oven floor. You are now ready to make a pizza.

3. Stretch out the dough as shown in "How to Shape a Pizza" (page 51). Lightly dust your pizza peel with flour. Place your stretched dough directly on the peel and proceed to build the pizza.

4. Brush the stretched dough with the remaining 1 tablespoon of garlic oil and spread the salsa bianca evenly over the dough, leaving a ½-inch border all the way around the outside. Arrange the shredded cheese evenly over the sauce, and top with the roasted red onions. Season the pie with a pinch of salt.

5. Quickly slice the artichokes as thinly as possible on a mandoline and place in a small bowl. Season with a few drops of olive oil and salt to inhibit burning while in the oven. Scatter evenly over the pizza.

6. Slide the pizza into the oven and bake for 3 to 5 minutes, rotating once or twice to ensure even cooking. Remove the pizza to a cutting board and slice into 6 or 8 wedges. Garnish with the thyme. Brush the crust edges with a quick pass of the garlic oil to finish.

WHAT TO DRINK: *I have heard it said that artichokes do not pair with any wine selection, red or white. Try a nicely chilled rosé and judge for yourself.*

ROASTED BUTTERNUT SQUASH, ROQUEFORT, AND WALNUT PIZZA

MAKES ONE 10-INCH PIZZA

Prep time: 30 minutes
Cook time: about 10 minutes

This may be the ultimate autumn pizza. Toasted nuts and robust sage accent a wonderful marriage of oven-roasted squash and pungent cheese. Thinly sliced, butternut squash cooks quickly, and the flesh isn't watery, like some other squash varietals. Roquefort is a French sheep's milk cheese that has a rich buttery flavor and gusto that can stand up to the strong oven heat even when melted.

½ butternut squash, peeled, seeded, and cut into ⅛-inch-thick slices

2 tablespoons Essential Garlic Oil (page 69), divided, plus more for finishing

Salt

1 portion Elevated Pizza Dough (page 52)

¼ cup shredded part-skim mozzarella

2 ounces Roquefort or domestic blue cheese, crumbled

Parmesan cheese

Freshly ground black pepper

¼ cup walnuts, toasted, skinned, and roughly chopped

1 bunch fresh sage, leaves picked and fried (see Prep Tip)

1. Toss the squash slices in 1 tablespoon of garlic oil and season with salt. Arrange on a half sheet pan in a single layer and roast in a medium-hot oven for 4 to 5 minutes or until lightly browned and tender. Allow the squash to cool before building the pie.

2. Following the directions for a fully prepped oven, make sure your fire is at the desired cooking temperature with a roiling flame and a brushed and cleaned oven floor. You are now ready to make a pizza. →

3. Stretch out the dough as shown in "How to Shape a Pizza" (page 51). Lightly dust your pizza peel with flour. Place your stretched dough directly on the peel and proceed to build the pizza.

4. Brush the stretched dough with the remaining 1 tablespoon of garlic oil and spread the shredded mozzarella evenly over the dough, leaving a ½-inch border all the way around the outside. Arrange the roasted squash slices so they don't overlap, and fill in the spaces with the crumbled Roquefort. Sprinkle the entire pie with a pinch of salt.

5. Slide the pizza into the oven and bake for 3 to 5 minutes, rotating once or twice to ensure even cooking. Remove the pizza to a cutting board, grate Parmesan cheese over the entire pie, and add a few grinds of black pepper. Crumble the walnuts over the pizza and arrange the whole fried sage leaves. Slice into 6 or 8 wedges. Brush the crust edges with a quick pass of the garlic oil to finish.

PREP TIP: *Frying herbs is a great way to add a crispy element to garnishes and still maintain an herbal flavor in the recipe. Heat about 2 inches of canola oil in a pot until it reaches 350°F on a thermometer. Quickly drop in the sage leaves and stand back! They will shudder and pop for a few seconds, then fry and deepen in color. After about 30 seconds remove with a slotted spoon to a paper towel–lined tray and season with salt. The oil can be cooled and used successive times to fry herbs.*

A GREEN PIE
ZUCCHINI, RAPINI, AND PESTO

MAKES ONE 10-INCH PIZZA
Prep time: 20 minutes
Cook time: about 10 minutes

I like to make pizzas that are visually appetizing as well as delicious. This variation on a color theme accomplishes both goals. Zucchini is plentiful when it finally arrives at the market; select multiple sizes and shades of green, and arrange them in an edible mosaic.

3 or 4 zucchini, thinly sliced on a mandoline

2 tablespoons Essential Garlic Oil (page 69), divided, plus more for finishing

Salt

1 bunch rapini

1 tablespoon extra-virgin olive oil

1 portion Whole-Wheat Pizza Dough (page 56) or Spelt Pizza Dough (page 54)

4 ounces fresh buffalo mozzarella, sliced into rounds

¼ cup Basic Pesto (page 74)

Parmesan cheese

1 teaspoon dried chili flakes

1. Toss the sliced zucchini in 1 tablespoon of garlic oil and season with salt. Chop the rapini and sauté in a covered pan in 1 tablespoon of olive oil, a splash of water, and a pinch of salt. Cook for 3 to 5 minutes. Allow to cool before building the pizza.

2. Following the directions for a fully prepped oven, make sure your fire is at the desired cooking temperature with a roiling flame and a brushed and cleaned oven floor.

3. Stretch out the dough as shown in "How to Shape a Pizza" (page 51). Lightly dust your pizza peel with flour. Place your stretched dough directly on the peel and proceed to build the pizza.

4. Brush the stretched dough with the remaining 1 tablespoon garlic oil and arrange the zucchini evenly over the dough, leaving a ½-inch border all the way around the outside. Spoon over the cooked rapini and top with the mozzarella. Drizzle the pesto over the pizza.

5. Slide the pizza into the oven and bake for 3 to 5 minutes, rotating once or twice to ensure even cooking. Remove the pizza to a cutting board, grate Parmesan cheese over the entire pie, and sprinkle on the chili flakes. Slice into 6 or 8 wedges. Brush the crust edges with a quick pass of the garlic oil to finish.

FRESH PORCINI MUSHROOM PIZZA

MAKES ONE 10-INCH PIZZA
Prep time: 30 minutes
Cook time: 15 minutes

Few wild mushrooms are more lauded than porcini, whether fresh or dried. Italians have an undying love affair with king boletes, as they are also known. Back in California, there are three distinctly different porcini mushroom seasons. Spring, summer, and fall can produce exceptional crops if conditions are favorable, so there is ample opportunity to enjoy this pizza almost year round. Porcini are expensive, so choose wisely. Select specimens that are dense, heavy for their size, and have white to tan undersides to the caps. Avoid spongy or slimy examples; they will have been out of the ground too long and are highly susceptible to bugs.

1 pound fresh porcini mushrooms

3 tablespoons Essential Garlic Oil (page 69), divided, plus more for finishing

Salt

1 portion Spelt Pizza Dough (page 54), Elevated Pizza Dough (page 52), or Basic Go-To Easy Pizza Dough (page 49)

4 ounces imported Fontina Val d'Aosta cheese, grated

Parmesan cheese

Freshly ground black pepper

2 tablespoons torn fresh mint leaves

1. Wipe the porcini free of any dirt that might still be attached with a damp towel and cut into ⅛-inch-thick slices. Toss the sliced mushrooms in 1 tablespoon of garlic oil and spread out in a single layer on a half sheet, then season with salt. Roast slowly in the window of the wood oven, 7 to 10 minutes. Allow to cool before building the pizza.

2. Following the directions for a fully prepped oven, make sure your fire is at the desired cooking temperature with a roiling flame and a brushed and cleaned oven floor. You are now ready to make a pizza.

3. Stretch out the dough as shown in "How to Shape a Pizza" (page 51). Lightly dust your pizza peel with flour. Place your stretched dough directly on the peel and proceed to build the pizza.

4. Brush the stretched dough with the remaining 2 tablespoons garlic oil and distribute the shredded Fontina evenly over the dough, leaving a ½-inch border all the way around the outside. Distribute the roasted mushrooms evenly. Season with a pinch of salt.

5. Slide the pizza into the oven and bake for 3 to 5 minutes, rotating once or twice to ensure even cooking. Remove the pizza to a cutting board, grate Parmesan cheese over the entire pie, and add a few grinds of black pepper. Scatter the torn mint over all. Slice into 6 or 8 wedges. Brush the crust edges with a quick pass of the garlic oil to finish.

SUBSTITUTION TIP: *Dried porcini have a deep, pungent, woodsy flavor that does not lend itself to this pizza, in my opinion. Resist using them and instead opt for another fresh wild mushroom or the excellent cultivated maitake, also known as "hen of the woods."*

MOREL MUSHROOM PIZZA WITH CREAM AND A SUNNY-SIDE UP EGG

MAKES ONE 10-INCH PIZZA
Prep time: 40 minutes
Cook time: about 25 minutes

Morel mushrooms are the true indication of the arrival of spring, from the Midwest to the Pacific Northwest. West of the Rocky Mountains they can be found in a range of habitats, but never more prolific than in forests that have previously suffered wildfire. Whenever I see morels in the market, they inevitably appear in that night's dinner. Their natural affinity for cream, eggs, and wood smoke make for a wonderful preparation if you are feeding a crowd and need to stretch these often-pricey mushrooms.

1 cup morel mushrooms, sliced, washed, and drained (see A Closer Look)
Salt
2 tablespoons unsalted butter
1 teaspoon chopped fresh thyme
3 thick asparagus spears
Extra-virgin olive oil
1 extra-large egg
1 portion Elevated Pizza Dough (page 52)
2 tablespoons Essential Garlic Oil (page 69), plus more for finishing
¼ cup shredded part-skim mozzarella
2 tablespoons heavy cream
Parmesan cheese
Freshly ground black pepper

1. Preheat a cast iron skillet large enough to hold the sliced morels in a single layer by placing it in a high-heat section of the oven for 5 minutes. Season the morels with a generous pinch of salt and add to the preheated skillet. Cook until all the liquid in the pan has evaporated and the mushrooms begin to sizzle rather than steam, 8 to 10 minutes. Stir in the butter and thyme and return the skillet to the oven for another 3 minutes. Remove and allow to cool until ready to build the pizza.

2. Prepare the asparagus by snapping off the woody stems and discarding. Using a mandoline, carefully slice the raw asparagus lengthwise, creating paper-thin ribbons. Toss the asparagus ribbons in a small bowl with a splash of olive oil and a pinch of salt.

3. Carefully crack the egg into a small bowl. Discard the watery layer that surrounds the white, taking care to keep the yolk intact.

4. Following the directions for a fully prepped oven, make sure your fire is at the desired cooking temperature with a roiling flame and a brushed and cleaned oven floor. You are now ready to make a pizza.

5. Stretch out the dough as shown in "How to Shape a Pizza" (page 51). Lightly dust your pizza peel with flour. Place your stretched dough directly on the peel and proceed to build the pizza.

6. Brush the stretched dough with the garlic oil and spread the shredded cheese evenly over the dough, leaving a ½-inch border all the way around the outside. Arrange the dressed asparagus ribbons over the dough, followed by the cooked morels. Drizzle the assembled pizza with the heavy cream and season the entire pie with a pinch of salt.

7. Slide the pizza into the oven and bake for 2 minutes to set the bottom of the crust. Remove the pie, carefully tip the cracked egg into the center of the pizza, and return it to the oven. Bake until the egg white is opaque but the yolk is still runny, another 2 to 3 minutes.

8. Remove the pizza to a cutting board, grate Parmesan cheese over the entire pie, and add a few grinds of black pepper. Slice into 6 or 8 wedges, being careful to cut around the unbroken yolk. Brush the crust edges with a quick pass of the garlic oil to finish. Enjoy the pizza by dunking a slice into the softly cooked egg yolk.

A CLOSER LOOK: *Morels can be a little tricky to work with. They may contain sand, ash, or even critters. Wash the mushrooms repeatedly in a bowl of tepid water, lifting them out with a strainer. Repeat the process with clean water until no more grit settles to the bottom of the bowl. Drain on a kitchen towel to help absorb the excess moisture. It is also very important that they are fully cooked before consuming, as they contain toxins that are mildly poisonous when eaten raw. Fortunately, the risk is eliminated with high-heat cooking.*

STINGING NETTLE AND CHANTERELLE MUSHROOM PIZZA

MAKES ONE 10-INCH PIZZA
Prep time: 35 minutes
Cook time: about 20 minutes

The first time I ate stinging nettles, it was an epiphany—so much complex flavor from a meager tangle of wilted greens. The first time I was stung was just as memorable: While stretching for a cluster of half-buried yellow chanterelles, I brushed against the spiked plant and saw stars! Revenge is a dish best served piping hot: Stinging nettle and chanterelle pizza became dinner. Before cooking, handle with care (and kitchen gloves). However, nettles lose their sting once they are cooked. Choose specimens that have thin central stalks and have not yet begun to flower, which means they have not yet formed tiny seed heads and small green beads.

2 cups stinging nettles, woody stems removed
8 ounces chanterelle mushrooms
Salt
3 tablespoons Essential Garlic Oil (page 69), divided, plus more for finishing
1 portion Basic Go-To Easy Pizza Dough (page 49)
½ cup Simple Tomato Sauce (page 70)
½ cup shredded part-skim mozzarella
1 tablespoon extra-virgin olive oil
Aged pecorino romano
Freshly ground black pepper

1. Fill a bowl with water large enough to hold the nettles, and soak them for 5 minutes. Agitate the nettles once or twice to loosen any dirt. Using tongs, lift them from the water, leaving the dirt behind, and drain thoroughly in a colander. Set aside until ready to use.

2. Wipe away any dirt that may still be attached to the chanterelle mushrooms. Slice them into small chunks of roughly the same size and follow the directions for cleaning mushrooms outlined for morels on page 161.

3. Following the directions for a fully prepped oven, make sure your fire is at the desired cooking temperature with a roiling flame and a brushed and cleaned oven floor.

4. Preheat a cast iron skillet, large enough to hold the sliced chanterelles in a single layer, by placing it in a high-heat section of the oven for 5 minutes. Season the chanterelles with a generous pinch of salt and add to the preheated skillet. Cook until all the liquid in the pan has evaporated and the mushrooms begin to sizzle rather than steam, 8 to 10 minutes. Remove the pan and add 1 tablespoon of garlic oil to the mushrooms, stirring to evenly coat, and cook for another 2 to 3 minutes. Remove from the oven and allow to cool until ready to build the pizza.

5. Stretch out the dough as shown in "How to Shape a Pizza" (page 51). Lightly dust your pizza peel with flour. Place your stretched dough directly on the peel and proceed to build the pizza.

6. Brush the stretched dough with the remaining 2 tablespoons garlic oil and spread the tomato sauce evenly over the dough, leaving a ½-inch border all the way around the outside. Arrange the shredded cheese, distributing evenly. Spread the cooked chanterelles over the cheese. In a small bowl, dress the nettles with 1 tablespoon of olive oil and a generous pinch of salt. Toss using kitchen tongs to avoid being stung. Pile the nettles on the pizza in a liberal heap.

7. Slide the pizza into the oven and bake for 3 to 5 minutes, rotating once or twice to ensure even cooking. Remove the pizza to a cutting board, shave the aged pecorino romano cheese over the entire pie, and add a few grinds of black pepper. Slice into 6 or 8 wedges. Brush the crust edges with a quick pass of the garlic oil to finish.

SUBSTITUTION TIP: *If nettles aren't available in your area, try growing your own—they take very quickly to most soil conditions and propagate actively. Lacinato kale can be substituted. If chanterelles are out of season, try using another wild mushroom. Avoid shiitake and portobello mushrooms at all costs—they aren't wild, and make a poor substitution flavor-wise.*

BLACK TRUFFLE AND FONTINA PIZZA

MAKES ONE 10-INCH PIZZA
Prep time: 25 minutes
Cook time: 3 to 5 minutes

I like the use of the Elevated Pizza Dough for this pizza; it pairs nicely with the northern Italian cheese and the deep, rich flavor of the black truffles. There is plenty going on here, despite the lack of a traditional sauce. The truffles are protected from the intense dry heat of the oven by the cheese, which acts as a vehicle for their heady aroma. I like to make this pie during the winter holiday season, when truffles are abundant and splurging on guests feels like the right thing to do.

8 ounces Yellow Finn potatoes, cut into ⅛-inch-thick slices

Salt

Extra-virgin olive oil

1 portion Elevated Pizza Dough (page 52)

2 tablespoons Essential Garlic Oil (page 69), plus more for finishing

1 fresh black truffle

4 ounces Fontina Val d'Aosta cheese, shredded

Parmesan cheese

Freshly ground black pepper

1. In a bowl, toss the potato slices with a generous pinch of salt and moisten with a splash each of olive oil and water. Arrange the potatoes in a single layer on a half sheet and roast in a very hot oven until they begin to take on color and soften, 4 to 7 minutes. Allow the potatoes to cool completely, taste, and adjust the seasoning with more salt if needed. Set aside until you're ready to build the pizza.

2. Following the directions for a fully prepped oven, make sure your fire is at the desired cooking temperature with a roiling flame and a brushed and cleaned oven floor. You are now ready to make a pizza.

3. Stretch out the dough as shown in "How to Shape a Pizza" (page 51). Lightly dust your pizza peel with flour. Place your stretched dough directly on the peel and proceed to build the pizza.

4. Brush the dough with the garlic oil and sprinkle a pinch of salt over the entire pie. Using a truffle slicer or a mandoline or a very sharp knife, slice the truffle as thinly as possible and cover the entire pie with the slices. Top the truffles with the Fontina, and add a few gratings of Parmesan over all.

5. Slide the pizza into the oven and bake for 3 to 5 minutes, rotating once or twice to ensure even cooking. Remove the pizza to a cutting board and add a few grinds of black pepper. Slice into 6 or 8 wedges. Brush the crust edges with a quick pass of the garlic oil to finish.

SUBSTITUTION TIP: *If your budget or the season doesn't allow for fresh black truffles, do not substitute truffle oil. This is a modern-day version of snake oil and generally contains unwanted artificial chemicals and the lowest quality truffles available—often harvested well outside the country of origin cited on the bottle. More often than not, the oil turns rancid before you can use it all, making the cost thoroughly unjustified.*

8 CALZONES AND SWEET HAND PIES

TAKE YOUR PIZZA-BUILDING SKILLS a step further, into stuffed crusts and folded doughs. The techniques that you have by now mastered by creating and shaping doughs can be applied to all manner of sweet and savory calzones. Baking these filled doughs requires a bit of attention to detail, and finding the right spot in the oven to simultaneously set the crust and finish the fillings. It is a good exercise in calculating relative hot and cool spots in your particular setup. Don't hesitate to go a little slower on the bake with these recipes; after all, you will not risk burning the fillings since they are shielded by a top layer of dough.

You'll find both savory and sweet recipes in this chapter. I call the sweet ones hand pies because they are small enough to eat with one hand and have the double crust of a pie.

In the earlier chapters I eschewed the use of a rolling pin to achieve a thin crust. In these recipes it may prove worthwhile to use one. If the dough is very elastic and won't hold its shape, cover with a kitchen towel and let it rest for five minutes. Remember, you and your guests will be enjoying crust top and bottom in each bite, so thinner is definitely better.

THREE-CHEESE CALZONE

MAKES ONE 8-INCH HALF-MOON CALZONE

Prep time: 5 minutes
Cook time: 7 to 10 minutes

You may never get past this calzone variation; its simplicity and charm is that great. A blend of three distinct cheeses that you can readily find in any supermarket, it won't break the bank either. The measure of a perfectly cheesy calzone is evidenced in the first bite. Mind the stretch of stringy cheese hanging from your chin!

 1 portion Basic Go-To Easy Pizza Dough (page 49)
 ¼ cup Simple Tomato Sauce (page 70)
 ¼ cup shredded part-skim mozzarella cheese
 2 ounces imported provolone, grated
 1 ounce goat cheese, crumbled
 1 tablespoon extra-virgin olive oil, plus more for finishing
 1 tablespoon chopped fresh flat-leaf parsley
 Salt
 Freshly ground black pepper

1. Following the directions for a fully prepped oven, make sure your fire is at the desired cooking temperature with a roiling flame and a brushed and cleaned oven floor. You are now ready to make a calzone.

2. Begin by dusting your work surface with a small amount of flour. Stretch the pizza dough by hand to a thin disc as described in "How to Shape a Pizza" (page 51). Dust the dough with a small amount of flour, turn over, and dust the other side. Using a rolling pin, gently roll the dough into a large, even, very thin circle. Continue to roll the dough, adding more flour as needed to prevent sticking. Transfer the dough to a lightly floured pizza peel.

3. Build the calzone on the half of the dough closest to you, as it will be folded over to create a half-moon shape. Spread the tomato sauce over the dough. Be sure to leave a 1-inch border to allow for a proper seal. Arrange the mozzarella, then the provolone, and finally the goat cheese over all. Drizzle the olive oil over the cheeses and sprinkle on the parsley. Season with salt and pepper. →

4. In one quick motion, grasp the upper, undressed portion of dough and fold it over to meet the opposite edge, creating a half moon. Starting at one edge, seal the dough by pinching and rolling it over onto itself. Continue until the calzone is sealed. Tear a 1-inch hole in the top of the dough to release steam when baking.

5. Slide the calzone directly onto the oven floor and bake, rotating once or twice, until it is nicely puffed and browned, 7 to 10 minutes. Remove from the oven and brush the entire calzone with a small amount of olive oil to give it a glossy shine.

SUBSTITUTION TIP: *Try any of the savory calzone preparations in this chapter with a variety of doughs from chapter 3. I like the Basic Go-To Easy Pizza Dough for this recipe, and the Elevated Pizza Dough or Whole-Wheat Pizza Dough for meat-filled calzones.*

THREE-MEAT CALZONE

MAKES ONE 8-INCH HALF-MOON CALZONE

Prep time: 15 minutes
Cook time: 7 to 10 minutes

This is a great way to use up those bits of charcuterie that are taking up room in your refrigerator. While no artisanal brands are needed to make this calzone shine, imported prosciutto trumps the domestic offerings, in my opinion. Seek out a reputable source for good pork products, preferably made in house, and preferably fed an organic diet. You'll taste the difference. Ask your butcher to slice all your meats as thinly as possible; thick prosciutto is as unpalatable as it is frivolous. For a delicious variation, omit the prosciutto from the interior and drape it over the warm, finished calzone for a contrasting taste to the cooked meats.

1 portion Basic Go-To Easy Pizza Dough (page 49)
¼ cup Simple Tomato Sauce (page 70)
¼ cup shredded part-skim mozzarella cheese
2 ounces pork sausage, crumbled and precooked (see Prep Tip)
2 ounces Genoa-style salami, cut into thin matchsticks
1 tablespoon chopped fresh flat-leaf parsley
1 teaspoon chopped fresh sage
Freshly ground black pepper
2 slices prosciutto
Extra-virgin olive oil

1. Following the directions for a fully prepped oven, make sure your fire is at the desired cooking temperature with a roiling flame and a brushed and cleaned oven floor. You are now ready to make a calzone.

2. Begin by dusting your work surface with a small amount of flour. Stretch the pizza dough by hand to a thin disc as described in "How to Shape a Pizza" (page 51). Dust the dough with a small amount of flour, turn over, and dust the other side. Using a rolling pin, gently roll the dough into a large, even, very thin circle. Continue to roll the dough, adding more flour as needed to prevent sticking. Transfer the dough to a lightly floured pizza peel. →

3. Build the calzone on the half of the dough closest to you, as it will be folded over to create a half-moon shape. Spread the tomato sauce over the dough. Be sure to leave a 1-inch border to allow for a proper seal. Layer the shredded cheese, followed by the sausage and salami. Toss the parsley and sage together and sprinkle over the fillings. Season with freshly ground pepper. Lay the prosciutto slices over the entire half-moon in one single layer.

4. In one quick motion, grasp the upper, undressed portion of dough and fold it over to meet the opposite edge, creating a half moon. Starting at one edge, seal the dough by pinching and rolling it over onto itself. Continue until the calzone is sealed. Tear a 1-inch hole in the top of the dough to release steam when baking.

5. Slide the calzone directly onto the oven floor and bake, rotating once or twice, until it is nicely puffed and browned, 7 to 10 minutes. Remove from the oven and brush the entire calzone with a small amount of olive oil to give it a glossy shine.

PREP TIP: *Remove the pork sausage from its casing, crumble, and bake in a cast iron skillet in the wood oven. Or, sauté it until rendered and crispy, about 5 minutes. Allow the mixture to cool completely before using inside the calzone.*

THREE-VEGETABLE CALZONE

MAKES ONE 8-INCH HALF-MOON CALZONE

Prep time: 40 minutes
Cook time: about 30 minutes

You have to eat your veggies, and this is a good respite if you have had your fill of salty meat pizzas and calzones. Unlike with the vegetable pizza recipes, it is a good idea to precook the ingredients here, because they will be tucked inside the dough. A quick sauté of the asparagus, radicchio roasted in the oven, and poached artichokes will ensure even cooking of the calzone.

3 thick asparagus spears

Extra-virgin olive oil

1 teaspoon salt, plus more for seasoning

1 head radicchio

1 tablespoon red wine vinegar

½ cup baby artichokes, prepared (see Prep Tip)

1 portion Basic Go-To Easy Pizza Dough (page 49)

¼ cup Simple Tomato Sauce (page 70)

¼ cup shredded part-skim mozzarella cheese

1 tablespoon chopped fresh flat-leaf parsley

Freshly ground black pepper

1. Snap the woody ends off the asparagus, and with a vegetable peeler remove some of the tough skin on the lower end of the spears. Cut the spears on the bias into 2-inch-long segments. Toss with a little olive oil and salt and roast in a small cast iron skillet for 2 to 3 minutes.

2. Quarter the head of radicchio and cut out the stem and core from the wedges. Cut each wedge crosswise into ½-inch-thick ribbons. Transfer to a bowl and toss with a little olive oil, the red wine vinegar, and 1 teaspoon of salt. Transfer to a cazuela and roast in the oven, turning and tossing, until wilted and somewhat browned, 5 to 7 minutes.

3. Drain and transfer the prepared artichokes to a cazuela, drizzle with olive oil and salt, add a splash of water, and roast in the window of the oven until tender, 5 to 7 minutes.

4. Following the directions for a fully prepped oven, make sure your fire is at the desired cooking temperature with a roiling flame and a brushed and cleaned oven floor. You are now ready to make a calzone. →

5. Begin by dusting your work surface with a small amount of flour. Stretch the pizza dough by hand to a thin disc as described in "How to Shape a Pizza" (page 51). Dust the dough with a small amount of flour, turn over, and dust the other side. Using a rolling pin, gently roll the dough into a large, even, very thin circle. Continue to roll the dough, adding more flour as needed to prevent sticking. Transfer the dough to a lightly floured pizza peel.

6. Build the calzone on the half of the dough closest to you, as it will be folded over to create a half-moon shape. Spread the tomato sauce over the dough. Be sure to leave a 1-inch border to allow for a proper seal. Next, layer the shredded cheese, followed by the asparagus, artichokes, and finally ½ cup roasted radicchio. Sprinkle the chopped parsley over the ingredients and add a few grinds of black pepper.

7. In one quick motion, grasp the upper, undressed portion of dough and fold it over to meet the opposite edge, creating a half moon. Starting at one edge, seal the dough by pinching and rolling it over onto itself. Continue until the calzone is sealed. Tear a 1-inch hole in the top of the dough to release steam when baking.

8. Slide the calzone directly onto the oven floor and bake, rotating once or twice, until it is nicely puffed and browned, 7 to 10 minutes. Remove from the oven and brush the entire calzone with a small amount of olive oil to give it a glossy shine.

PREP TIP: *Prepare the artichokes by removing the tough outer leaves, trimming the stems, and slicing in half. Using a small spoon, scoop out the fibrous "choke" if there is one. Cut the artichoke in half again and transfer to a bowl of water that contains the juice of 1 lemon. Repeat until all the artichokes are cleaned.*

THE ACROPOLIS
SPINACH, FETA, TAPENADE, AND OREGANO

MAKES ONE 8-INCH HALF-MOON CALZONE

Prep time: 20 minutes
Cook time: 7 to 10 minutes

1 portion Basic Go-To Easy Pizza Dough (page 49)

¼ cup Tapenade (page 78)

¼ cup part-skim mozzarella cheese, shredded

2 ounces feta cheese, drained and crumbled

1 cup spinach leaves, stems removed

1 red onion, thinly sliced on a mandoline, dressed with olive oil and salt

1 tablespoon pine nuts, lightly toasted

1 teaspoon oregano, oven-dried (see Prep Tip on page 145) or fresh

Freshly ground black pepper

Extra-virgin olive oil

One of the things I miss about the East Coast is the abundance of all-night diners. Open 24 hours a day, seven days a week, they were always there, like a beacon for the late-night reveler and truck driver alike. These diners were mostly owned by Greek families, and I would marvel at the scope of the menu, which would inevitably include a few specialties from the islands—Americanized, of course. Here is a calzone for the generation of Greeks who fed me day or night.

1. Following the directions for a fully prepped oven, make sure your fire is at the desired cooking temperature with a roiling flame and a brushed and cleaned oven floor. You are now ready to make a calzone.

2. Begin by dusting your work surface with a small amount of flour. Stretch the pizza dough by hand to a thin disc as described in "How to Shape a Pizza" (page 51). Dust the dough with a small amount of flour, turn over, and dust the other side. Using a rolling pin, gently roll the dough into a large, even, very thin circle. Continue to roll the dough, adding more flour as needed to prevent sticking. Transfer the dough to a lightly floured pizza peel. →

3. Build the calzone on the half of the dough closest to you, as it will be folded over to create a half-moon shape. Spread the tapenade over the dough. Be sure to leave a 1-inch border to allow for a proper seal. Next, layer the mozarella and feta cheeses, followed by the spinach, red onion, and pine nuts. Sprinkle the oregano over the filling and season with freshly ground pepper.

4. In one quick motion, grasp the upper, undressed portion of dough and fold it over to meet the opposite edge, creating a half moon. Starting at one edge, seal the dough by pinching and rolling it over onto itself. Continue until the calzone is sealed. Tear a 1-inch hole in the top of the dough to release steam when baking.

5. Slide the calzone directly onto the oven floor and bake, rotating once or twice, until it is nicely puffed and browned, 7 to 10 minutes. Remove from the oven and brush the entire calzone with a small amount of olive oil to give it a glossy shine.

STUFFED AND ROLLED PIZZA RING

MAKES ONE 10-INCH RING CALZONE

Prep time: 20 minutes
Cook time: 7 to 10 minutes

Stuffed pizzas can be just as fun to make as they are to eat. All manner of fillings work well— bearing in mind that they should be kept to a minimum, as with pizzas. Here, a ring is chosen for simplicity, when you are building pies and feeding a crowd simultaneously. Be sure to roll the dough thinly, and then have fun with ingredients and funky shapes.

1 portion Basic Go-To Easy Pizza Dough (page 49)

2 tablespoons Essential Garlic Oil (page 69)

½ cup Simple Tomato Sauce (page 70)

¼ cup shredded part-skim mozzarella cheese

½ cup crumbled, cooked fennel sausage (see Prep Tip on page 172)

2 tablespoons grated pecorino romano

1 teaspoon oregano, oven-dried (see Prep Tip on page 145) or fresh

Salt

Freshly ground black pepper

Extra-virgin olive oil

1. Following the directions for a fully prepped oven, make sure your fire is at the desired cooking temperature with a roiling flame and a brushed and cleaned oven floor. You are now ready to make a calzone.

2. Begin by dusting your work surface with a small amount of flour. Stretch the pizza dough by hand to a thin disc as described in "How to Shape a Pizza" (page 51). Dust the dough with a small amount of flour, turn over, and dust the other side. Using a rolling pin, thinly roll the dough into a 10-inch round, adding more flour as needed to prevent sticking. Transfer the dough to a lightly floured pizza peel. →

3. To build the ring, spread the garlic oil evenly over the dough, followed by the tomato sauce. Next, layer the shredded mozzarella, followed by the crumbled sausage, and then the pecorino romano. Sprinkle the oregano over the filling and season with salt and black pepper.

4. Starting at one edge, roll up the dough as if you're making a jelly roll and seal the edges by pinching them down. Turn the entire log over so the seam side is down. Gather both ends and connect them by lightly pinching together. Shape into a ring, taking care not to over-handle the dough or puncture it. Clean the peel of any ingredients that might prevent it from easily sliding in the oven.

5. Slide the ring directly onto the oven floor and bake, rotating once or twice and moving the ring through hot and cool zones to get even browning, until it is nicely puffed and browned, 7 to 10 minutes. Remove from the oven and brush the entire ring with a small amount of olive oil to give it a glossy shine. Allow to cool slightly before cutting into wedges.

SCHIACCIATA ALL'UVA
WINE GRAPE FOCACCIA

MAKES ONE 12-BY-16-INCH FLATBREAD
Prep time: 2 hours
Cook time: 20 to 30 minutes

1 recipe Rosemary Focaccia (page 62), reducing the fresh rosemary to ¼ cup

3 cups fresh wine grapes, such as Zinfandel or Pinot Noir or Concord, stemmed

Flaked sea salt

In the fall, when the wine grapes ripen, the tradition was to celebrate the season's harvest by creating all manner of festive dishes using the fruit. The ritual of baking plump wine grapes into doughy focaccia has been around for centuries, and reinforces the concept of sweet and sour, or *agrodolce*. I like to use our American grape staple, Zinfandel. However, Concord grapes also work well in this recipe if wine grapes are not readily available where you live. I don't fret over the grape seeds; they provide a characteristic crunch. *Schiacciata* is a classic Tuscan flatbread, typically cooked in the ashes of the hearth. The name literally means "squashed."

1. After you have topped the focaccia dough with the olive oil and rosemary, distribute the wine grapes evenly over the entire pan and gently press into the dough. The schiacciata is now ready for the oven.

2. To bake the schiacciata, allow a medium-hot fire to burn down so it is no longer flaming. A nice mass of glowing embers and a fully heated oven is best. A slow steady bake is ideal here to prevent over-browning. If you have a laser thermometer, you are looking for a floor temperature of around 425°F. Insert the half sheet opposite the fire source and bake until the schiacciata is puffed and deep golden. Approximately 20 minutes of baking should set the dough; depending on your fire, it may take another 10 minutes.

3. Remove the pan from the oven and allow it to cool slightly. With a sharp knife cut around the dough and release it from the pan in one slab. The parchment paper should still be on the baked schiacciata, but if it isn't, don't fret. →

4. Slide the dough back onto the warm oven floor for a final bake of the dough. This ensures a nice, evenly crispy crust. If you feel your schiacciata is sufficiently baked to your liking, omit this final step. Top with a generous sprinkling of flaky salt.

5. Transfer to a cooling rack. When cool, invert and peel off the parchment paper. I like to cut my schiacciata into large wedges or rectangular "fingers" that I can wrap in a napkin and pass to my guests as they enjoy a glass of wine.

A CLOSER LOOK: *When cooking a flatbread, I like to rotate the pan frequently. This does two things: It allows me to check the progress of the bake and also gauge the fire's intensity. Too cool and I add a small piece of wood; too hot and I can cover the dough loosely with a piece of heavy aluminum foil to slow the browning on the surface.*

SWEET HAND PIE OF PUMPKIN, WARM SPICES, AND MASCARPONE

MAKES TWO 6-INCH HAND PIES
Prep time: 45 minutes, plus overnight for chilling
Cook time: 6 to 8 minutes

If you plan on making your own pumpkin purée for this recipe, go with what's known as a sugar pumpkin. While I have never found them to be any sweeter than other varietals of gourds, I like the small size and flesh-to-seed ratio, and they tend to be a bit less watery. Make a large batch, season, and freeze the extra. In general, I find that the canned versions of pumpkin, organic if you can find it, are surprisingly delicious and not too wet. Choose pumpkin purée, not pumpkin pie filling, which is already sweetened and spiced. Adding vanilla extract, a splash of bourbon, and a pinch of salt brightens the flavor even more.

1 recipe Sweet Dough for Hand Pies (page 64)
½ cup pumpkin purée
¼ teaspoon ground nutmeg
¼ teaspoon ground cinnamon
Pinch ground cloves
1 teaspoon pure vanilla extract
2 tablespoons bourbon (optional)
½ cup mascarpone cheese
¼ cup granulated sugar, plus more for topping the pie
Salt
1 egg yolk
1 tablespoon whole milk
½ cup (1 stick) unsalted butter, melted
Powdered sugar (optional)

1. Wrap the dough and shape into a thin, flat rectangle. This will make rolling the chilled dough easier. Chill overnight in the refrigerator. The next day, roll the dough on a lightly floured surface and cut into two 5½-by-4¼-inch rectangles. Chill or freeze until ready to use.

2. In a medium bowl, combine the pumpkin purée with the nutmeg, cinnamon, cloves, vanilla, and bourbon, if using. In another bowl, combine the mascarpone and the granulated sugar and stir to dissolve.

3. Arrange a piece of dough with the shorter side closest to you. Spread half of the sweetened cheese on the bottom half of the dough, leaving a 1-inch margin from the edge of the dough. Top the mascarpone with half of the pumpkin mixture. Sprinkle on a pinch of salt.

4. Whisk together the egg yolk and milk. Brush the three exposed edges of the dough with the egg wash and fold the top half of the dough over the filling. Seal by pressing lightly with the back of a fork. Brush the entire pastry with melted butter and sprinkle over a little granulated sugar. With a sharp knife, make a slash or two on the top of the pie to release steam. Repeat with the other pie.

5. Refrigerate both pies for at least 15 minutes or up to 4 hours before baking.

6. Transfer the pies to a floured peel and bake in a moderate oven until the pastry is well colored and the filling is warmed through, 6 to 8 minutes. Cool slightly before enjoying. Dust with powdered sugar if desired.

PREP TIP: *Make the sweet dough two days before you plan to use it. The day before, roll out the dough in a rectangle using a rolling pin. Measure two 5½-by-4¼-inch pieces with a ruler, cut with a knife, and refrigerate or freeze until ready to use.*

SWEET HAND PIE OF ROASTED STONE FRUITS AND FRANGIPANE

MAKES TWO 6-INCH HAND PIES
Prep time: 45 minutes, plus overnight for chilling
Cook time: 6 to 8 minutes

The early summer brings my favorite fruits of the year: plums, pluots, apricots, nectarines, cherries, and peaches. The ripening crop almost overwhelms. The fast-expiring fruit can be used up in a frangipane hand pie. Frangipane is a mixture of ground almonds, butter, sugar, and eggs. You can buy frangipane, but it's much better if you make it yourself (see A Closer Look). Make sure you start with pure almond paste, not marzipan.

1 recipe Sweet Dough for Hand Pies (page 64)
1 pound fresh stone fruits
1 vanilla bean, split, seeds scraped out
¼ cup granulated sugar, plus more for topping the pie
2 tablespoons frangipane
2 tablespoons sliced almonds, toasted
1 egg yolk
1 tablespoon whole milk
½ cup (1 stick) unsalted butter, melted
Powdered sugar (optional)

1. Wrap the dough and shape it into a thin, flat rectangle. This will make rolling the chilled dough easier. Chill overnight in the refrigerator. The next day, roll the dough on a lightly floured surface and cut into two 5½-by-4¼-inch rectangles. Chill or freeze until ready to use.

2. Cut the fruit in half and remove the pits. Cut each half into 2 or 3 wedges, or more if the fruit is large. Transfer to a bowl and add the vanilla seeds and granulated sugar. Toss to combine. Transfer to a cazuela and roast in a hot oven until soft, bubbly, and slightly colored, 3 to 5 minutes. Do not overcook the fruit to the point where it entirely breaks down. Taste and adjust with more sugar if needed. Cool completely before using.

3. Arrange a piece of dough with the shorter side closest to you. Spread half of the frangipane on the bottom half of the dough, leaving a 1-inch margin from the edge of the dough. Top with ¼ cup roasted stone fruit and 1 table-spoon sliced almonds.

4. Whisk together the egg yolk and milk. Brush the three exposed edges of the dough with the egg wash and fold the top half of the dough over the filling. Seal by pressing lightly with the back of a fork. Brush the entire pastry with melted butter and sprinkle over a little granulated sugar. With a sharp knife, make a slash or two on the top of the pie to release steam. Repeat with the other pie.

5. Refrigerate both pies for at least 15 minutes or up to 4 hours before baking.

6. Transfer to a floured peel and bake in a moderate oven until the pastry is well colored and the filling is warmed through, 6 to 8 minutes. Cool slightly before enjoying. Dust with powdered sugar if desired.

A CLOSER LOOK: *To make frangi-pane, beat ½ cup (1 stick) unsalted butter using the paddle attachment of an electric stand mixer. Slowly add 8 ounces almond paste and beat on high speed until smooth and blended. Beat in 2 tablespoons granulated sugar, 1 tablespoon all-purpose flour, and 1 large egg. Beat for 1 minute more, until light and airy and thoroughly combined. Refrigerate until needed. Frangipane will keep for up to 1 week in the refrigerator or 2 months in the freezer.*

SWEET HAND PIE OF ROASTED CHERRIES WITH GRAPPA AND AMARETTI

MAKES TWO 6-INCH HAND PIES
Prep time: 45 minutes, plus overnight for chilling
Cook time: 6 to 8 minutes

1 recipe Sweet Dough for Hand Pies
(page 64)

1½ pounds fresh cherries

1½ tablespoons grappa (optional)

1 vanilla bean, split, seeds scraped out

¼ cup granulated sugar, plus more for
topping the pie

Salt

2 tablespoons frangipane (see A Closer
Look on page 185)

3 tablespoons amaretti cookie crumbs

1 egg yolk

1 tablespoon whole milk

½ cup (1 stick) unsalted butter, melted

Powdered sugar (optional)

In the mid-to-late spring in California, the organic cherry crop starts to arrive at the market, but before that I will often be driving through the central valley on the way to the Sierra Nevada to forage for morels. As the foothills begin to loom in the close distance, I begin scanning the empty lots I pass at seventy miles an hour, looking for a lawn chair, an umbrella, a few stacked fruit crates, and a poorly worded sign advertising cherries. It is always just outside a dusty farm town that I eat my first cherries of the spring. Truth be told, they are not as good as they will be in the coming weeks, but I can't resist. There's something about cherry pit spitting and hunting morel mushrooms that goes together.

1. Wrap the dough and shape it into a thin, flat rectangle. This will make rolling the chilled dough easier. Chill overnight in the refrigerator. The next day, roll the dough on a lightly floured surface and cut into two 5½-by-4¼-inch rectangles. Chill or freeze until ready to use.

2. Stem and pit the cherries and toss with the grappa, if using, the vanilla bean pod and seeds, and the granulated sugar. Add a pinch of salt. Transfer to a cazuela and roast the cherries until they soften and become slightly syrupy, about 5 minutes. Stir once or twice to

avoid burning the fruit. Allow to cool before making the hand pies. Discard the vanilla bean pod. You should end up with about ½ cup cooked cherries.

3. Arrange a piece of dough with the shorter side closest to you. Spread half of the frangipane on the bottom half of the dough, leaving a 1-inch margin from the edge of the dough. Spread half of the cooked cherries and top with half of the amaretti crumbs.

4. Whisk together the egg yolk and milk. Brush the three exposed edges of the dough with the egg wash and fold the top half of the dough over the filling. Seal by pressing lightly with the back of a fork. Brush the entire pastry with melted butter and sprinkle over a little granulated sugar. With a sharp knife, make a slash or two on the top of the pie to release steam. Repeat with the second pie.

5. Refrigerate both pies for at least 15 minutes or up to 4 hours before baking.

6. Transfer to a floured peel and bake in a moderate oven until the pastry is well colored and the filling is warmed through, 6 to 8 minutes. Cool slightly before enjoying. Dust with powdered sugar if desired.

A CLOSER LOOK: *Amaretti are small, sweet Italian cookies that are made using sweet and bitter almonds. They are quite dry and retain their crunch even when pulverized. The best come from the town of Saronno; you can find them at Italian specialty grocers. Grappa is an intense, high-alcohol liquor created from the remnants of wine-making, whereby the pressed seeds, stems, and skins of grapes are distilled. Grappa can be purchased at well-appointed liquor stores. Expect to pay a premium for better bottles.*

SWEET HAND PIE OF BLISTERED APRICOTS, RICOTTA, AND BITTERSWEET CHOCOLATE

MAKES TWO 6-INCH HAND PIES

Prep time: 45 minutes, plus overnight for chilling
Cook time: 6 to 8 minutes

Apricots and wood smoke make for an ideal marriage; the sunny sweetness contrasts with the fire-roasted char. Burnt sugar is the effect you are after in this recipe, so be sure to sugar the fruit well and set it right next to the embers. Roast the fruit when you have a minute between pizzas, when the oven is fully engaged and the flames are licking at the dome.

1 recipe Sweet Dough for Hand Pies (page 64)

1 pound fresh apricots

¼ cup granulated sugar, plus more for topping the apricot halves and pies

1 vanilla bean, split, seeds scraped out

¼ cup plus 2 tablespoons fresh whole-milk ricotta cheese

3 tablespoons roughly chopped bittersweet chocolate

3 tablespoons toasted, chopped unsalted pistachios

1 egg yolk

1 tablespoon whole milk

½ cup (1 stick) unsalted butter, melted

Powdered sugar (optional)

1. Wrap the dough and shape it into a thin, flat rectangle. This will make rolling the chilled dough easier. Chill overnight in the refrigerator. The next day, roll the dough on a lightly floured surface and cut into two 5½-by-4¼-inch rectangles. Chill or freeze until ready to use.

2. Split the apricots in half and remove the pits. Arrange in a cazuela, cut-side up, and top with a sprinkle of granulated sugar, a splash of water, and the vanilla bean pod and seeds. Roast the fruit next to the coals in a very hot oven so the cooking goes quickly and color develops rapidly. I don't mind a little char on the fruit in this case. Discard the vanilla bean pod.

3. Combine the ricotta and the granulated sugar and stir to dissolve. Fold in the chocolate. Chill until ready to use.

4. Arrange a piece of dough with the shorter side closest to you. Spread half of the sweetened cheese on the bottom half of the dough, leaving a 1-inch margin from the edge of the dough. Top with 2 or 3 blistered apricot halves, cut-side down. Sprinkle over half of the chopped pistachios.

5. Whisk together the egg yolk and milk. Brush the three exposed edges of the dough with the egg wash and fold the top half of the dough over the filling.

Seal by pressing lightly with the back of a fork. Brush the entire pastry with melted butter and sprinkle over a little granulated sugar. With a sharp knife, make a slash or two on the top of the pie to release steam. Repeat with the second pie.

6. Refrigerate both pies for at least 15 minutes or up to 4 hours before baking.

7. Transfer to a floured peel and bake in a moderate oven until the pastry is well colored and the filling is warmed through, 6 to 8 minutes. Cool slightly before enjoying. Dust with powdered sugar if desired.

A CLOSER LOOK: *There are so many boutique chocolates on the market these days, it is hard to tell what is worth the money without trying them all. My advice is to go middle-of-the-road and buy bittersweet, at least 70 percent cocoa.*

9 BEYOND PIZZA

THE WOOD OVEN HAS ENDLESS POSSIBILITIES when it comes to menu ideas. In this chapter we will explore a variety of cooking techniques, from slow cooking to high-heat roasting and even grilling. There are a multitude of hot environments created in a wood-burning oven, so let's use them all.

You will need to expand somewhat on the skill set you have developed while working with pizza doughs and live fire. These recipes call for techniques away from the wood oven, such as frying crèpes or making fresh pasta, to prepare dishes that will ultimately be finished in the wood oven.

I urge you to hold the same regard for the ingredients listed here that you did when shopping for flours, olive oil, and the like. Get to know your local fishmongers and butchers. If they have stands at your local farmers' markets, so much the better to do one-stop shopping. Many businesses have a social media presence to connect with their customers, so you can get on their product e-mail lists and be the first to get prized ingredients before they come to market.

Since salads are the perfect pairing for pizza, I've also included four inventive salads at the end of this chapter, each highlighting a different season.

WOOD-FIRED SHEEP'S MILK RICOTTA

MAKES 2 CUPS
Prep time: 10 minutes
Cook time: 10 to 15 minutes

Artisanal cheese makers across the country have rediscovered the simplicity and thrift of making fresh ricotta. Heating and acidulating the leftover whey from cow- and sheep-milk cheese production, they efficiently turn a by-product into a delicious add-on product.

1 pound fresh sheep's milk ricotta
½ cup extra-virgin olive oil
1 tablespoon salt
Freshly ground black pepper
Zest of 1 lemon, grated
½ cup Wild Fennel Sauce (page 77)
    (optional)

1. In a food processor, purée the ricotta, olive oil, salt, pepper, and lemon zest until smooth and whipped. Taste and adjust the seasoning as needed.

2. Spoon into a cazuela and smooth the top. Add the fennel sauce, if using, and spread evenly over the top of the smoothed cheese.

3. Bake in a moderate oven until lightly puffed and slightly browned on top, 10 to 15 minutes. Remove and let cool.

4. At this point the ricotta can be cut into wedges or spooned onto toasts or flatbread and served as an appetizer.

WARM MONTRACHET WRAPPED IN GRAPE LEAVES WITH ROASTED WINE GRAPES AND FLATBREAD

SERVES 6 AS AN APPETIZER
Prep time: 10 minutes
Cook time: 4 to 5 minutes

2 (7-ounce) logs Montrachet or similar goat cheese
4 fresh grape leaves, washed and dried
1 large cluster wine grapes
1 tablespoon extra-virgin olive oil
Salt
North African Flatbread (page 60)

Soft, ripe goat cheese, wrapped in grape leaves and warmed in the hearth, is an ideal ending (or beginning) to a meal. If you have leftover wine grapes from the recipe for Schiacciata all'Uva (page 179), roast a cluster and serve them with flatbread for a seasonal fall appetizer.

1. Wrap the grape leaves around the goat cheese and tuck in the loose ends. Transfer to a cazuela and set in the window of the oven. Roast just until softened and easily spreadable—it won't take long.

2. At the same time, toss the grape cluster with the olive oil and season with a bit of salt. Roast in a cast iron skillet for 4 to 5 minutes.

3. Enjoy the cheese and fruit paired with the crisp flatbread.

OVERNIGHT OVEN-DRIED TOMATOES SOTT'OLIO

MAKES 1 QUART

Prep time: 10 minutes
Cook time: overnight

After a full pizza cooking session where the oven has had a chance to heat and cook for several hours, there will be plenty of residual heat left over for some overnight oven-drying projects. Capture the stored heat of the oven's masonry to dry these tomatoes. If your oven has a tight fitting door, you will need it. If not, cover the opening of the oven with a half sheet pan. Salt the halved tomatoes and place on a cooling rack to slightly drain for 30 minutes before placing them in the oven. The salt helps draw out some of the moisture before they go in the oven for drying.

2 pounds ripe tomatoes, such as Early Girl or Roma, halved, salted, and drained (see Prep Tip below)

Salt

Fresh herbs, such as rosemary, thyme, and oregano

3 cups extra-virgin olive oil

1. When the oven has significantly cooled after a cooking session, rake the fire to break it up further. There should no longer be any flames and very few, if any, glowing coals. Allow the heat to dissipate for a few minutes.

2. Arrange as many half sheet pans as you like. Line them with cooling racks and place the tomatoes, cut-side up, snugly next to one another. Place the pans inside the cooling oven and set the door in place.

3. The next morning, retrieve the dehydrated, concentrated tomatoes and transfer to clean, dry mason jars. Pack the tomatoes fairly tightly, layering with herbs of your choice. Omit any tomatoes that have burned.

4. Cover the dried tomatoes with the olive oil and, using a chopstick or other utensil, try to release any trapped air among the layers by moving the tomatoes around so the oil fills the spaces where the air may have become trapped. Screw the lid on tightly and transfer to the refrigerator.

5. Over time the tomatoes will soften and the oil will take on the delicious flavor of the herbs and fruit. Enjoy both as part of an antipasto plate, on grilled bread, and of course on pizza.

GRATIN OF WILD MUSHROOM CRÈPES

MAKES 12 CRÈPES

*Prep time: 10 minutes for the crèpes, 10 minutes
for the filling, plus overnight for chilling*

*Cook time: 30 minutes for the crèpes, 5 minutes
for the filling*

Crèpes are a great vehicle for serving all manner of ingredients. Guests will be impressed that you made them from scratch, and only you will know just how easy it was. Make the batter the day before, to allow the gluten in the flour to relax overnight in the refrigerator. The following morning, cook the crèpes, then wrap the entire stack tightly in plastic wrap until ready to use.

FOR THE CRÈPES

2 cups whole milk

¼ cup (½ stick) unsalted butter

Salt

1¾ cups all-purpose flour

4 extra-large eggs

¼ cup beer (optional)

Canola oil

FOR THE FILLING

1½ pounds wild mushrooms such as porcini, morels, chanterelles, or black trumpets

Salt

4 tablespoons (½ stick) unsalted butter, divided, plus more for the cazuela

4 tablespoons extra-virgin olive oil, divided

1 recipe Salsa Bianca (page 75)

2 garlic cloves, minced

2 tablespoons chopped fresh thyme

½ cup heavy cream

½ cup grated Parmesan cheese

TO MAKE THE CRÈPES

1. In a small saucepan, warm the milk and butter together until the butter melts. Add a pinch of salt and set aside to cool slightly.

2. In the bowl of an electric stand mixer fitted with the whisk attachment, whisk the flour on low speed, then add the eggs all at once. Increase the speed to medium and whisk until combined and no lumps or flour remain visible. Lower the speed and slowly add the warm milk mixture, whisking constantly until combined.

3. Strain the batter through a fine-mesh strainer, pushing through any solids that remain. If the batter seems very thick, thin it with a few tablespoons of beer (if using) or milk. It should have the consistency of pancake batter. Refrigerate overnight.

4. Stir the crêpe batter well to combine anything that may have settled overnight. Grease a nonstick skillet or crêpe pan with a small amount of canola oil and heat over medium heat. Add 1 to 1½ ounces batter; simultaneously tilt and swirl the pan to get an even, thin pancake. Cook for 2 minutes, then flip the crêpe using a spatula or your fingers and cook for 30 seconds longer.

5. Slide the crêpe out of the pan, reheat the pan, and repeat until all of the batter has been used. Stack the cooked crêpes on top of one another and wrap in plastic wrap until ready to use, or freeze for up to 2 months.

TO MAKE THE FILLING

1. Clean and slice the mushrooms. Transfer to a dry kitchen towel to help absorb the excess moisture.

2. Cook the mushrooms in four small batches so they sauté rather than steam. Season each batch with salt, and as the liquid they give off evaporates, add 1 tablespoon each of butter and oil per batch. Cook until they start to crisp and caramelize slightly, a few minutes longer. Remove to a plate and repeat with the other mushrooms, until all are cooked.

3. Transfer the mushrooms to a bowl and stir in enough salsa bianca to evenly coat them. Add the garlic and thyme.

4. Butter a large cazuela. Fill each crêpe with an equal amount of mushroom filling and fold over into a wedge. Transfer to the buttered pan. Lean each crêpe on the previous one to create a shingled pattern. Drizzle over the heavy cream and sprinkle the Parmesan cheese over all.

5. Bake in a moderately hot oven until the crêpes crisp, the cheese melts, and the filling is warmed through, about 5 minutes.

EGGPLANT ROASTED IN THE COALS

MAKES 1 CUP
Prep time: 10 minutes
Cook time: 30 to 40 minutes

2 medium globe eggplants

2 garlic cloves, mashed

2 tablespoons chopped fresh
 flat-leaf parsley

1 tablespoon chopped fresh mint

2 teaspoons ground coriander

1 teaspoon ground cumin

Salt

Freshly ground black pepper

½ cup extra-virgin olive oil

Juice of 1 lemon

Roasting vegetables in their jackets, in hot coals, is a technique that allows their inherent moisture to stay intact. This type of cooking works well for all manner of foods; try potatoes wrapped in thick foil or beets or even celery root bulbs put directly on embers. When cooked, you simply peel away the burnt outside skin to reveal a smoky flesh that doesn't require dirtying a bunch of pots and pans. This dish is delicious as an appetizer, spread on the North African Flatbread (page 60).

1. Carefully fill a cast iron skillet with glowing embers. Using a metal peel works best to lift and deposit them into the pan. Place the eggplants directly in the coals in the skillet. Roast until very soft and blackened, 30 to 40 minutes, depending on their size, turning every so often.

2. Carefully remove the cooked eggplant to a heat-resistant tray and allow to cool until reasonable to handle.

3. Peel away the outer skin and scoop the flesh into a bowl. Or, if you prefer a smooth consistency, purée the flesh in a food processor.

4. Add the garlic, parsley, mint, coriander, cumin, salt, and pepper. Drizzle in the olive oil and balance the richness with the lemon juice and/or more salt.

ROASTED WINTER VEGETABLES IN DUCK FAT AND ROSEMARY

SERVES 6 AS A SIDE DISH
Prep time: 30 minutes
Cook time: 10 to 20 minutes

In the winter months it can be tough to add variety to the dinner table, especially if you rely on growing some of your own food, local farmers' markets, or seasonal shopping. Turn to root vegetables for an easy accompaniment. These dense, hearty vegetables offer a wide variety of preparations, from long-cooked gratins to purées and everything in between. Mixing them all together in duck fat and herbs, then roasting until caramelized will brighten any dreary winter night.

1 celery root, peeled and cut into 1-inch chunks

3 large parsnips, peeled and cut into 1-inch chunks

4 large carrots, peeled and cut into 1-inch chunks

12 small Tokyo turnips, or 1 large turnip, cut into 1-inch chunks

1 bulb fennel, cut into 1-inch chunks

¼ cup duck fat, melted

3 fresh rosemary sprigs, leaves stripped from the woody stems

Salt

1. Place the cut celery root, parsnips, carrots, turnips, and fennel in a bowl large enough to toss easily. Add the duck fat and rosemary, toss to thoroughly coat, season well with salt, and spread in a single layer on a half sheet pan.

2. Roast the vegetables in a moderate oven, rotating frequently and stirring to avoid burning, until they are tender, 10 to 20 minutes.

LONG-COOKED "POT O' BEANS"
WITH OKRA, TOMATOES, AND PEPPERS

MAKES 4 CUPS OF BEANS
Prep time: 20 minutes
Cook time: 1 hour 10 minutes

One-pot cooking is sometimes a requirement when using the wood oven, since space limitations and proximity to the fire mean real estate is at a premium. More importantly, flavors are layered and cooked together in combination with wood smoke. These beans are delicious over toasted bread.

8 tablespoons extra-virgin olive oil, divided

1 bay leaf

2 fresh thyme and/or savory sprigs

2 whole garlic cloves, peeled

3 cups fresh (or dried) shell beans such as cranberry, cannellini, or flageolet

½ yellow onion, cut in half

1 small fennel bulb, cut into 1-inch pieces

1 carrot, peeled and cut in half

1 cup okra, cut into 2-inch pieces

2 tomatoes, peeled, seeded, and diced

4 Jimmy Nardello peppers or 2 red bell peppers, seeded and diced

Salt

¼ cup chopped fresh flat-leaf parsley or basil

1. In a 4-quart pot, heat 2 tablespoons of olive oil on the stovetop, add the bay leaf and thyme or savory, then the garlic, and sauté gently for 30 seconds. Add the shell beans, onion, fennel, and carrot. Cover with water by 1 inch and bring to a boil. Lower the heat and slowly simmer until the vegetables are tender, 30 to 40 minutes.

2. Remove the cooked fennel and carrot and transfer the rest of the bean mixture to a cast iron pot with a tight-fitting lid. Add the okra, tomatoes, and peppers. Season with salt and add the remaining 6 tablespoons of olive oil, plus ½ cup to 1 cup water if the liquid level is low. Cover and place inside the doorway of the wood oven, next to the fire. Slowly cook until the tomatoes dissolve, the peppers are tender, and the okra has thickened the broth, 20 to 30 minutes.

3. Garnish with chopped fresh parsley or basil.

PREP TIP: *If you're using fresh shell beans, cook them ahead of time, reserving the savory broth. Mix the cooked beans with the broth, okra, tomatoes, and pepper to speed up cooking time in the oven and free up floor space.*

SHAKSHUKA

BAKED EGGS WITH TOMATOES AND DUKKA

SERVES 6
Prep time: 20 minutes
Cook time: 12 to 15 minutes

This Israeli breakfast has been gaining in popularity recently, and why not? It makes a satisfying, easy-to-prepare meal any time of the day. Dukka is a fragrant Middle Eastern blend of nuts, spices, and seeds. There are a variety of blends and no two are quite the same, but all seem to include at least coriander and sesame. Look for dukka online or at better specialty food stores. It seems these days everyone is raising chickens at home, so there is an ample supply of fresh eggs to be had. Depending on how your birds produce, things can get out of hand in a hurry. This dish will knock a dent in the hen-house production—yours or your neighbor's.

2 tablespoons extra-virgin olive oil
1 yellow onion, diced
4 ripe tomatoes, roughly chopped
2 garlic cloves, minced
Salt
6 eggs
1 tablespoon chopped fresh flat-leaf parsley
Freshly ground black pepper
1 tablespoon dukka (optional)

1. Heat a cast iron skillet in the oven for 5 minutes, add the olive oil, and sweat the onion until soft and transparent. Add the chopped tomatoes and garlic and season with salt. Cook the tomatoes and onions until they concentrate and break down somewhat, 7 to 10 minutes, stirring occasionally.

2. Remove the pan from the oven and make 6 shallow depressions in the tomato-onion mixture. Crack the eggs individually into each depression and season with salt. Return to the oven and bake slowly until the whites are opaque and set and the yolks are runny, about 5 minutes. Garnish with chopped parsley, black pepper, and dukka, if using. Enjoy with toast.

SHRIMP COOKED IN THE WOOD OVEN WITH GARLIC AND OIL

SERVES 4 AS AN APPETIZER

Prep time: 20 minutes

Cook time: 3 to 5 minutes

The simplicity of this dish and the fine results it produces are reason enough to explain why it is on most menus at the checkered-tablecloth red sauce Italian joints. There is no shame in enjoying this much garlic on shrimp, just don't confuse this with true Italian cooking.

1 pound fresh shrimp, peeled and deveined

4 garlic cloves, pounded to a paste in a mortar and pestle

½ cup extra-virgin olive oil

Salt

Freshly ground black pepper

1 teaspoon chili flakes

½ cup (1 stick) unsalted butter, cut in small pieces

¼ cup dry white wine

Juice of 1 lemon

¼ cup chopped fresh flat-leaf parsley

1. In a large bowl, toss the shrimp with the garlic and oil. Season with salt, a few grinds of black pepper, and the chili flakes. Arrange the shrimp in a cazuela, dot with butter, and pour over the white wine.

2. Transfer the prepared cazuela to a hot oven and roast until the shrimp are opaque and cooked through, 3 to 5 minutes. Remove from the oven, squeeze the lemon juice over the dish, and garnish with the chopped parsley.

SUBSTITUTION TIP: *This dish is exceptional if you have access to spot prawns, which are very sweet but have a short season. It becomes something you might find on a Venetian menu where the shellfish is fresh from the Adriatic Sea.*

CRACKED LOBSTERS ROASTED WITH PAPRIKA BUTTER

MAKES 2 LOBSTERS
Prep time: 30 minutes
Cook time: 5 to 7 minutes

This recipe brings together the wood-burning fire and high-quality crustaceans. When you combine the two, the results are transcendent—especially when they're basted in a highly seasoned compound butter of garlic and two kinds of paprika. Be sure to offer a crusty loaf of bread alongside—and lots of napkins.

2 whole live Maine lobsters

1 pound (4 sticks) unsalted butter, at room temperature

1 tablespoon sweet paprika

1 tablespoon smoked paprika

2 garlic cloves, smashed

Zest and juice of 2 limes

2 teaspoons salt

1 tablespoon cognac

1. Kill the lobsters by plunging a very sharp knife through the heads and set aside for 10 minutes in a bowl until they stop moving. Remove the claws and tail, reserving the body for another use.

2. In a pot of boiling water, cook the tails for 3 minutes and the claws for 5. Remove to a bowl filled with ice water. Drain and dry.

3. Split the tails in half, leaving the meat in the shell. Remove the knuckles from the claws and, with a small mallet, crack the shells all over.

4. Make the compound butter in the bowl of an electric stand mixer fitted with the paddle attachment. First soften the butter by beating it on medium speed for 3 minutes, then add both paprikas,

the garlic, lime zest and juice, salt, and cognac, and beat until smooth. Taste and adjust with more of everything, if needed.

5. Spread the shellfish out in a single layer on a half sheet pan. Smear three-quarters of the soft compound butter over the meat and shells, working it into the cracks made by the mallet.

6. Roast the shellfish until it is sizzling and lightly colored, 5 to 7 minutes. Remove to a bowl and melt the reserved compound butter. Serve the lobster with the extra compound butter.

SUBSTITUTION TIP: *I use this recipe with great results for our local Dungeness crabs (two of them, boiled for 12 minutes), spiny lobsters (two, boiled for 6 minutes), and jumbo spot prawns (a dozen, cut in half lengthwise, no need to boil), when their respective seasons come around.*

WHOLE ROASTED BRANZINO WITH TOMATOES, POTATOES, AND WHITE WINE

SERVES 4

Prep time: 25 minutes
Cook time: 20 to 30 minutes

2 large Yellow Finn potatoes, peeled and cut into ½-inch dice

12 fresh rosemary sprigs, divided

2 whole (1½-pound) branzino, cleaned

Salt

Freshly ground black pepper

1 lemon, thinly sliced

½ cup extra-virgin olive oil, divided

½ cup (1 stick) unsalted butter, cut in small pieces, divided

1 cup dry white wine, divided

½ cup cherry tomatoes

½ cup fish or chicken stock

¼ cup chopped fresh flat-leaf parsley

Whole roasted branzino (sea bass) is visually stunning, both before it goes into the oven and when it emerges. I am enamored with the process of cooking fish on the bone; it retains more moisture and is flavored by herbs and citrus stuffed in the cavity. Ask your fishmonger to clean the whole fish for you, or do it yourself. This amounts to scaling, removing the gills, and emptying the stomach cavity. Clip the side fins as well. By all means ask that the head be left on; for that matter, don't ever buy headless whole fish as it is a sign that the fish may be past its prime.

1. Cook the potatoes in boiling salted water until tender, about 10 minutes. Drain well and reserve.

2. On a half sheet pan, scatter 8 of the rosemary sprigs. Season the inside of the fish cavities with salt and pepper, and stuff each with 2 rosemary sprigs and the lemon slices. Drizzle with ¼ cup of olive oil.

3. Season the outside of the fish with salt and pepper and place on top of the rosemary-lined sheet tray. Drizzle the entire platter with the remaining ¼ cup of olive oil. Dot with half of the unsalted butter, and pour over ½ cup of white wine.

4. Bake in a moderately hot oven, at least 500°F, rotating frequently and sliding closer to the mouth should the fish begin to darken too quickly. After 10 minutes, remove the tray and scatter the cherry tomatoes and cooked potatoes around and about the fish. Return to the oven and cook until the fish is somewhat translucent near the backbone, another 10 to 20 minutes.

5. When done, use a large spatula to remove the branzino to a waiting platter, scatter the vegetables around, and discard the rosemary branches from the pan.

6. Add the remaining ½ cup of wine, the remaining butter, and the stock to the pan, and use a wooden spoon to scrape up any bits that may have become stuck. Return the pan to the oven to heat through and reduce slightly. Add the chopped parsley to the sauce.

7. For each fish, remove the top fillet, then the spine, and finally the bottom fillet. Dig the cheek flesh out of the head, just below the eye. Serve with the roasted vegetables and pan sauce poured over.

A CLOSER LOOK: *Branzino is currently being farmed in a sustainable way. Be sure to ask your supplier the origins and practices of how the fish you are selecting were caught or raised.*

PASTA AL FORNO
CANNELLONI WITH SPINACH, LEEKS, AND CHICKEN

SERVES 4

*Prep time: 30 minutes for the pasta, 30 minutes
    for the cannelloni*
Cook time: 25 minutes

Pasta al forno means "pasta baked in the oven." There are dozens, perhaps hundreds, of oven-roasted pasta dishes, and cooking pasta in the wood oven must be as old as the Seven Hills of Rome. In this recipe, fresh pasta dough comes together quickly but requires a pasta machine to achieve the proper thinness. There is nothing like homemade pasta, but if you don't have a pasta machine, you can buy sheets of fresh pasta. Use it the day you buy it.

FOR THE PASTA

1 cup 00 flour

1 extra-large egg plus 1 extra-large
    egg yolk

1 tablespoon extra-virgin olive oil

FOR THE CANNELLONI FILLING

3 tablespoons unsalted butter, divided

2 tablespoons water

1 cup thinly sliced leeks

1½ pounds ground chicken

Salt

4 cups spinach leaves

2 cups Salsa Bianca (page 75)

1 cup shredded part-skim
    mozzarella, divided

½ cup heavy cream, divided

1 cup grated Parmesan cheese

Freshly ground black pepper

TO MAKE THE PASTA

1. Put the flour in the bowl of an electric stand mixer fitted with the paddle attachment. Add the egg, egg yolk, and olive oil and mix on low speed until the dough comes together. If it seems too dry, add a few drops of water.

2. Turn the dough out onto a lightly floured countertop and knead until it forms a slightly sticky ball. Wrap tightly in plastic wrap and let rest for 30 minutes.

3. Cut the dough ball in half and cover one half with plastic wrap. Using a pasta machine, gradually sheet the dough on the second to last setting on your machine, to retain an "al dente" bite after cooking. Repeat with the second half of the dough.

TO MAKE THE CANNELLONI

1. In a large sauté pan, melt 2 tablespoons of the butter with the water and sweat the leeks over medium heat until tender and transparent, 8 to 10 minutes. Add the ground chicken and cook thoroughly, about 5 minutes. Season with salt and transfer to a large bowl to cool.

2. Sauté the spinach in the remaining 1 tablespoon of butter until wilted, remove to a plate, and allow to cool. Squeeze out any excess moisture and roughly chop.

3. When the chicken is cool, add the Salsa Bianca and ½ cup of mozzarella. Mix well. Add the cooked spinach.

4. Bring a large pot of salted water to a boil. In the meantime, cut the sheeted pasta into eight 6-by-5-inch pieces. Have a bowl of ice water standing by and lay out a few clean towels on your kitchen counter. Cook the pasta sheets, a few at a time, for 2 to 3 minutes. Lift out with a large slotted spoon and drop into the ice water, then transfer to the towels and pat dry. Repeat the process until all the sheets have been cooked.

5. Gather a portion of the filling and roll it up in a pasta sheet, creating a tube. Wet the edges and seal. Transfer to a cazuela large enough to hold all eight cannelloni side by side, seam-side down. Repeat until all the pasta sheets and filling are used.

6. Brush some of the heavy cream over the rolled and filled pasta to moisten them and top with the Parmesan cheese and the remaining ½ cup of mozzarella. Season with salt and black pepper. Drizzle the remaining cream over the finished pasta rolls.

7. Bake in a moderately hot oven until the cheese melts and the pasta begins to brown and turns crispy, about 7 minutes.

8. Serve two cannelloni per person and spoon over the reduced cream.

VIETNAMESE-STYLE PORK SKEWERS IN LETTUCE CUPS

MAKES 10 TO 15 SKEWERS
Prep time: 30 minutes, plus overnight to marinate
Cook time: 5 to 7 minutes

These skewers come together quickly after they have marinated overnight. Exotic spices and flavors are at play here, so have plenty of cold beer on hand. Five-spice is a blend that is commonly used in Asian cooking and consists primarily of fennel, clove, star anise, cinnamon, and Sichuan pepper. Fresh galangal is a tough rhizome, much like the more common ginger root, and adds a similar flavor to Asian-style cooking. Kaffir lime leaves are the small green leaves from the citrus fruit tree of the same name. The leaves lend a perfume to cooked dishes throughout Asia; they can be used either fresh or dried and also freeze very well. Kaffir leaves, fish sauce, galangal, and five-spice can all be found in better Asian grocery stores. If you don't have one nearby, look online.

¼ cup nuoc cham (Vietnamese fish sauce)

¼ cup minced fresh lemongrass, ground finely in a food processor

¼ cup chopped garlic

¼ cup peeled and grated galangal

¼ cup minced shallot

4 kaffir lime leaves

2 Thai bird or serrano chiles, sliced

2 tablespoons freshly ground black pepper

1 tablespoon sugar

1 tablespoon Thai five-spice powder

2 pounds boneless pork shoulder

15 lettuce leaves

½ cup torn fresh cilantro leaves

¼ cup finely chopped peanuts

2 limes, cut into wedges

1. In a large bowl, combine the nuoc cham, lemongrass, garlic, galangal, shallot, kaffir lime leaves, chiles, black pepper, sugar, and five-spice powder.

2. Trim away any excess fat and gristle from the pork. Using a sharp knife, cut the pork into long, thin slices and add to the bowl. Mix the pork and the marinade well by hand. Cover with plastic wrap and refrigerate overnight.

3. The next day, remove the pork from the refrigerator at least 2 hours before you plan to cook it. Soak 15 wooden skewers in water for 1 hour.

4. Thread the pork slices onto the skewers. Transfer the skewers to a half sheet pan with the exposed wooden handles all facing the same direction. Do not overcrowd the skewers on the pan. When all the skewers are assembled, cover the exposed wooden handles with a sheet of aluminum foil to keep them from burning.

5. Transfer the skewers to the oven with the meat facing the fire. Cook until the pork browns and sizzles, remove from the oven, and use tongs to flip the skewers over. Return the protective foil to the handles and finish cooking on the other side. Cook for 5 to 7 minutes total.

6. Slide the skewers out of the pork and discard. Tuck each portion of pork into a lettuce cup, garnish with the cilantro and peanuts, and serve with a lime wedge.

SUBSTITUTION TIP: *Pork shoulder is a cheap cut that has great marbling of the fat. I do not mind that it has a bit of a chew to it for this dish, but feel free to use any cut of pork you prefer. The key is that it is cut very thin.*

RIB-EYE STEAK GRILLED "IN THE WINDOW" WITH SALSA VERDE

SERVES 2 AS A MAIN COURSE
Prep time: 1 hour
Cook time: about 15 minutes

Grilling in your pizza oven? Why not? There are several options on the market for short-legged stainless steel or cast iron grill grates that fit snugly in the oven window. Begin with a pizza session, then rake a bed of hot coals underneath the grill and produce charbroiled results without ever getting out the Weber. If you can, add vine cuttings to the fire for a special flavor; four or five 8-inch-long twigs will do. Reach for the rare Super Tuscan red you have been saving for a special occasion.

2 tablespoons black peppercorns, crushed

1 (24-ounce) grass-fed, bone-in rib-eye or porterhouse steak, at room temperature

1 tablespoon salt

2 fresh rosemary sprigs, leaves stripped from the woody stems

2 tablespoons extra-virgin olive oil

1 recipe Salsa Verde (page 76)

1. Season the meat liberally with the salt and crushed peppercorns, pressing them into the flesh. Add the rosemary and rub the steak with the olive oil. Let it rest for 30 minutes.

2. Slide the grill into the mouth of the oven and rake a glowing, not flaming, bed of coals underneath the grill grate. Allow the grill to preheat for 10 minutes. Ideally, there will be a hotter section and a relatively cooler section of the grill; you will use both. Add the vine cuttings (if you have them) to the existing fire, away from the grill, to create smoke and flame while grilling.

3. Place the steak on the hottest part of the grill and leave for about 3 minutes to form a nice crust. Rotate the steak 90 degrees and continue to grill for 2 minutes longer. Flip the steak and repeat.

4. After 5 minutes, pull the steak to the cooler mouth area and grill a bit more slowly to your desired doneness. Medium-rare to rare is ideal, which will be about 15 minutes total. (By all means, grill the steak the way you like it.)

5. Remove the steak to a platter and allow to rest for 5 minutes before carving off the bone and slicing against the grain into ¾-inch-thick strips.

6. Garnish with the salsa verde and serve.

OVEN-ROASTED FRUITS

SERVES 4
Prep time: 10 minutes
Cook time: 5 to 7 minutes

All manner of fruits are improved when roasted in the wood-fired oven. Here are just a few examples. All will work well on their own or as fillings for sweet hand pies. Don't stop here, though—whole roasted apples, pears in sweet wine, and even strawberries are a delight when fire-roasted.

FIGS ROASTED ON FIG LEAVES

2 fig leaves, washed and dried

8 fresh ripe figs, such as black Mission or Adriatic, stemmed and halved

2 tablespoons Chartreuse liqueur (optional)

2 tablespoons sugar

1. In a cazuela, arrange the fig leaves and top with the cut fruit, stem ends pointing upward. Choose a vessel that fit the figs snugly, as this will prevent them from drying out. Add the liqueur, if using, and sprinkle on the sugar.

2. Roast in a moderate oven until softened and juicy, 5 to 7 minutes. Serve with cheese, over ice cream, or alone.

CHERRIES ROASTED WITH KIRSCH AND CINNAMON

2 cups cherries, stemmed

2 tablespoons sugar

1 teaspoon ground cinnamon

2 tablespoons Kirsch (optional)

1. In a bowl, combine the cherries, sugar, cinnamon, and Kirsch, if using.

2. Transfer to a cazuela and roast in a moderate oven, stirring once or twice to prevent burning, 5 to 7 minutes. Tell your guests to mind the pits!

APRICOTS ROASTED WITH DESSERT WINE AND VANILLA BEANS

8 apricots, halved and pitted

½ cup dessert wine, such as Sauternes or Beaumes de Venise

¼ cup sugar

2 vanilla beans, split

1. In a cazuela, arrange the apricots, cut-side up. Pour over the dessert wine and sprinkle the sugar on top. Nestle the vanilla beans in and around the fruit.

2. Roast in a very hot oven for 5 to 7 minutes. Enjoy alone or in a sweet hand pie.

ESCAROLE, PERSIMMON, AND POMEGRANATE SALAD WITH TOASTED WALNUT VINAIGRETTE

SERVES 6 TO 8

Prep time: 30 minutes
Cook time: 5 to 7 minutes

Cooler fall weather is ideal for growing hearty chicories. A little bitter, a touch sweet, they pair nicely with seasonal fruits and new crop nuts. Choose dense heads of escarole, and use only the pale, greenish-white interior. If you can't find escarole, try using hearts of romaine lettuce. They lack the bitterness of escarole but provide all the crunch. If Fuyu persimmons are not available, use a crisp apple, sliced very thin. Leave the skin on the fruit for a contrast in taste, texture, and color.

1 cup shelled walnuts

Salt

6 teaspoons walnut oil, divided

1 shallot, minced

2 tablespoons Champagne vinegar

2 large heads escarole

2 cups arugula

3 heads Belgian endive, leaves separated and thinly sliced on the bias

1 tablespoon Dijon mustard

½ cup extra-virgin olive oil

2 Fuyu persimmons, peeled and very thinly sliced

1 cup pomegranate seeds (optional)

Freshly ground black pepper

Parmesan cheese (optional)

1. Preheat the oven to 350°F.

2. Toast the walnuts on a baking sheet until light brown, 5 to 7 minutes. Wrap in a clean, dry dish towel and vigorously rub off the skins. Carefully remove the nuts from the towel and discard the skins. While the nuts are still warm, season with a pinch of salt and 2 teaspoons of walnut oil, and mix thoroughly. Set aside until ready to use.

3. In a small bowl combine the shallot with a generous pinch of salt and cover with the vinegar. Set aside for 10 minutes.

4. In a large bowl, toss together the escarole, arugula, and endive. Cover with a dish towel and refrigerate until ready to serve.

5. Add the mustard to the shallots and vinegar. Gradually whisk in the remaining 4 teaspoons of walnut oil, followed by the olive oil, in a slow, steady stream. Adjust the seasoning with more salt, vinegar, or olive oil as needed.

6. Remove the chilled chicories from the refrigerator and add the sliced persimmons and half of the seasoned walnuts. Sprinkle over the pomegranate seeds (if using), and gently and briefly mix the salad using both hands. Add half of the vinaigrette and toss again.

7. Taste a bit of all the components and adjust accordingly with more salt, oil, or vinegar. Garnish with the remaining nuts, give it a grind of black pepper, and shave wide ribbons of Parmesan cheese over the entire salad if you like. Pass the remaining vinaigrette for guests to enjoy.

SIMPLE ARUGULA AND HERB SALAD

SERVES 6 TO 8
Prep time: 10 minutes

This is an ideal salad to enjoy with individual calzones. The citrus dressing stands up to the double dough and three cheeses. It's delicious as a stand-alone salad as well. Meyer lemons are becoming available nationwide and are incredibly delicious in all manner of preparations, from pickling to desserts. The juice of these brightly colored lemons is up to five times sweeter than a standard lemon, and its zest has a dusty, perfumed scent.

1 pound arugula

2 tablespoons fresh lemon juice (from Meyer lemons, if available)

Salt

Freshly ground black pepper

⅓ cup extra-virgin olive oil

1 bunch fresh mint, leaves torn into rough pieces

15 fresh anise hyssop leaves, torn into rough pieces (optional)

1. Put the arugula in a bowl large enough to facilitate tossing and dressing. Cover with a dish towel or damp paper towel and refrigerate until ready to use.

2. Put the lemon juice in a small bowl. Add a generous pinch of salt and several grinds of pepper. Whisk in the olive oil in a slow, continuous stream. Adjust the dressing with more salt or lemon juice. It should be bright and citrusy.

3. When ready to serve, sprinkle a generous pinch of salt over the arugula and add the mint and hyssop (if using). Toss by hand to distribute evenly. Drizzle half of the vinaigrette over the arugula and toss again until lightly coated. There should be no excess vinaigrette in the bottom of the bowl.

4. Taste and adjust with more salt or dressing as needed. Serve with the remaining vinaigrette on the side for guests to add to their liking.

FARM STAND VEGETABLE SALAD

SERVES 6 TO 8

Prep time: 30 minutes

Growing up in the Garden State, there was always an abundance of roadside farm stands to visit when school was on summer break. They seemed to pop right up out of the cornfields, a fresh coat of paint over ramshackle plywood. The hand-drawn signs advertised bumper crop prices, enticing drivers to pull over and spend a little money. Sadly, as urban sprawl devours farmland, these outposts are dwindling. Support your local farmers. If you can't find everything listed here, omit some or most of these ingredients—a ripe tomato salad still stands out as delicious.

1 shallot, minced

2 tablespoons Champagne vinegar

Salt

½ cup fresh green and/or purple basil leaves, plus 1 whole sprig

6 large, ripe tomatoes

1 large cucumber, peeled, seeded, and thinly sliced

2 large sweet peppers, cored and very thinly sliced

1 pint firm cherry tomatoes

⅓ cup extra-virgin olive oil

3 whole salt-packed anchovies, rinsed, soaked, and filleted (see Prep Tip on page 122)

1 cup Aïoli (page 79), thinned with 1 tablespoon water

Freshly ground black pepper

1. Put the shallot in a small bowl, cover with the vinegar, and add a generous pinch of salt and the basil sprig. Let stand for 10 to 15 minutes.

2. Cut the large tomatoes crosswise into ¼-inch-thick slices and arrange on a wide, flat platter. Collect any tomato juice that may have escaped during slicing and spoon it over the slices. Season the tomato layer with salt.

3. In a large bowl, toss together the sliced cucumber and peppers, season with a pinch of salt, and scatter them over the tomato slices. Halve the cherry tomatoes, season with a pinch of salt, and let stand while you make the vinaigrette.

4. Remove and discard the macerated basil sprig from the shallots and vinegar. Whisk in the olive oil. Spoon the dressing over the entire vegetable platter. Scatter with the halved cherry tomatoes and their juice.

5. Slice the anchovy fillets lengthwise and distribute evenly over the salad.

6. Finally, tear the basil leaves into 1-inch pieces and garnish the platter. Drizzle the aïoli over all of the vegetables and herbs, or serve it on the side for guests to dress their own salads. Finish with a few grinds of black pepper.

LACINATO KALE SALAD WITH CREAMY GARLIC DRESSING AND RADISHES

SERVES 6 TO 8
Prep time: 30 minutes
Cook time: about 5 minutes

Lacinato kale, also known as Tuscan kale or dinosaur kale, presumably for its prehistoric appearance, makes for a delicious and healthy winter salad. Briefly steaming the kale for a minute or two softens it, but it still retains its color and nutrition. I prefer to strip the leaves from the stems, which can be fibrous and tough.

3 bunches Lacinato kale, stems removed

1 egg yolk

1 teaspoon water

1 cup extra-virgin olive oil

Juice of 1 lemon

¼ cup cream

Salt

2 garlic cloves, mashed to a paste in a mortar and pestle

2 whole salt-packed anchovies, rinsed, soaked, filleted (see Prep Tip on page 122), and mashed to a purée in a mortar and pestle

1 cup grated pecorino romano cheese, divided

Freshly ground black pepper

½ cup sliced French breakfast radishes

1. Set up a pot with a tight-fitting lid and a steamer basket large enough to hold the kale after it has been washed and stripped from its stems. Add just enough water to reach below the bottom of the basket. Don't overcrowd the steamer; rather, work in several small batches if necessary and steam the kale for about 2 minutes, until all the kale has been barely wilted. Remove the kale to a dry dish towel and allow to cool and drain. Transfer the kale to a bowl suitable for dressing the salad and refrigerate until ready to use.

2. In a clean bowl, whisk together the egg yolk and water. Slowly add the olive oil, whisking constantly to create a thick mayonnaise and adding a squeeze of lemon juice to thin the mixture from time to time. When all of the oil has been added, whisk in the cream, a generous pinch of salt, the mashed garlic, and the anchovy purée. Adjust the mixture with a few drops of water. It should taste bright and acidic. The dressing should have the consistency of pancake batter—thin it with a bit more cream or a few drops of lemon juice if necessary.

3. Set the dressing aside for 5 minutes to allow the flavors to mingle, then add half of the grated cheese and a generous amount of black pepper. Refrigerate until ready to use.

4. When ready to serve, toss the kale with a generous pinch of salt, add just enough garlic dressing to evenly coat the leaves, and toss again. Add half of the remaining cheese and toss again. Garnish with the remaining cheese, a few grindings of black pepper, and the sliced radishes.

REFERENCES

Clark, Sam and Sam. *Moro East*. London: Ebury Press, 2011.

David, Elizabeth. *Italian Food*. Revised ed. New York: Penguin, 1999.

Hellmich, Mittie. *The Ultimate Bar Book*. San Francisco: Chronicle Books, 2006.

Italian Academy of Cuisine. *La Cucina: The Regional Cooking of Italy*. New York: Rizzoli, 2009.

Kallas, John. *Edible Wild Plants*. Layton, Utah: Gibbs Smith, 2010.

Locatelli, Giorgio. *Made In Italy: Food & Stories*. New York: HarperCollins, 2007.

Riley, Gillian. *The Oxford Companion to Italian Food*. New York: Oxford University Press, 2007.

Robertson, Chad. *Tartine Bread*. San Francisco: Chronicle Books, 2010.

Rubino, Roberto. *Italian Cheese*. 2nd ed. Cuneo, Italy: Slow Food Editore, 2005.

Silver Spoon Kitchen, *The Silver Spoon New Edition*. New York: Phaidon Press, 2011.

Waters, Alice. *Chez Panisse Café Cookbook*. New York: HarperCollins, 1999.

MEASUREMENT CONVERSIONS

Volume Equivalents (Liquid)

US STANDARD	US STANDARD (OUNCES)	METRIC (APPROXIMATE)
2 tablespoons	1 fl. oz.	30 mL
¼ cup	2 fl. oz.	60 mL
½ cup	4 fl. oz.	120 mL
1 cup	8 fl. oz.	240 mL
1½ cups	12 fl. oz.	355 mL
2 cups or 1 pint	16 fl. oz.	475 mL
4 cups or 1 quart	32 fl. oz.	1 L
1 gallon	128 fl. oz.	4 L

Oven Temperatures

FAHRENHEIT (F)	CELSIUS (C) (APPROXIMATE)
250°F	120°C
300°F	150°C
325°F	165°C
350°F	180°C
375°F	190°C
400°F	200°C
425°F	220°C
450°F	230°C

Volume Equivalents (Dry)

US STANDARD	METRIC (APPROXIMATE)
⅛ teaspoon	0.5 mL
¼ teaspoon	1 mL
½ teaspoon	2 mL
¾ teaspoon	4 mL
1 teaspoon	5 mL
1 tablespoon	15 mL
¼ cup	59 mL
⅓ cup	79 mL
½ cup	118 mL
⅔ cup	156 mL
¾ cup	177 mL
1 cup	235 mL
2 cups or 1 pint	475 mL
3 cups	700 mL
4 cups or 1 quart	1 L

Weight Equivalents

US STANDARD	METRIC (APPROXIMATE)
½ ounce	15 g
1 ounce	30 g
2 ounces	60 g
4 ounces	115 g
8 ounces	225 g
12 ounces	340 g
16 ounces or 1 pound	455 g

RECIPE INDEX

INDEX

ACKNOWLEDGMENTS

It is with an abundance of gratitude that I would like to thank the hard working, talented and openhearted contributors to this book. The generosity, knowledge and spirit that you applied to this project was truly enlightening and shaped my vision for what this book could be.

Firstly, to Frances Baca and the production team at Callisto Media, including everyone behind the scenes that encouraged me and felt my enthusiasm, a grand thank you. My editor Talia Platz, for allowing me to embrace this project as I saw it and provide me with endless support when I needed it.

Special thanks to the generosity of Tim Crosby and Robin Terra for allowing us to invade your wonderful home and overstay our welcome.

Thank you to Dan Brody, Amelia Lindbergh, and Cedric Tolosa for interpreting my vision of wood-fired cookery. The future is delicious and bright with you all behind the stoves.

Editors Beth Heidi Adelman and Karen Wise, thank you for taking a cook's ideas and simplifying them.

Thank you Katy Brown for your wonderful design elements throughout this book.

Thank you, Thomas Harder, for your invaluable knowledge and lengthy conversations on all things wood, you are an old soul.

The Eierman's, Colby, Megan, Peter, and Henry for sharing in the fun and food.

Joy Brace and HLC Company Goods for your stylish handmade kitchenware.

Thank you chef Amy Dencler and Sky Vineyards, and Aaron and Monica at The Local Butcher Shop for providing perfect ingredients.

John and Jess Sward for their artisan stonemason skills.

Author Darra Goldstein for your support and kind words; you inspire me greatly.

A final thanks to the amazingly talented duo of photographer Kelly Ishikawa and stylist Rod Hipskind.

ABOUT THE AUTHOR

ANTHONY TASSINELLO has spent the last two decades cooking at the iconic Chez Panisse restaurant in Berkeley, California and foraging for wild mushrooms from Oregon to Italy. A passion for wood-fired cookery, baking and pastry, and cocktail culture keeps him busy all four seasons. He was the foraging guide for author/food activist Michael Pollan in his acclaimed bestseller *The Omnivore's Dilemma*. His work has appeared in the *New York Times Magazine*, *SF Magazine*, the *Huffington Post*, NPR, and a variety of cookbooks. He calls Northern California home along with his girlfriend Frances, her son Bruno, and their orange cat Rooney.

Printed in the USA
CPSIA information can be obtained
at www.ICGtesting.com
LVHW060731301123
764704LV00003B/34